SAMS
Teach Yourself
Today

e-Genealogy

SAMS Teach Yourself Today

e-Genealogy

Finding Your Family Roots Online

Terri Stephens Lamb

SAMS

A Division of Macmillan USA
201 West 103rd Street, Indianapolis, Indiana 46290

Sams Teach Yourself e-Genealogy Today

International Standard Book Number: 0-672-31816-4

Library of Congress Catalog Card Number: 99-067008

Printed in the United States of America

First Printing: December 1999

01 00 99   4 3 2 1

Trademarks

Warning and Disclaimer

Acquisitions Editor
Jeff Schultz

Development Editor
Ned Snell

Managing Editor
Charlotte Clapp

Project Editor
Carol Bowers

Copy Editor
Kim Cofer

Indexer
Eric Schroeder

Proofreaders
Mary Ellen Stephenson
Tim Ryan

Team Coordinator
Amy Patton

Interior Designer
Gary Adair

Cover Designer
Jay Corpus

Copy Writer
Eric Bogert

Production
Dan Harris
Tim Osborn
Staci Somers
Mark Walchle

Dedication

For my family: I remember...

And for Dave, my best friend and brightest light.

Table of Contents

Foreword

Genealogy and technology meet at an unlikely crossroads. In the past, it was the halfway point between two very distant cultures, and people who were comfortable with one discipline were often very unfamiliar with the other. As a consequence, a speech or book addressing genealogy and technology was seldom presented to a single audience, but rather to two very distinct ones: persons who were skilled genealogists but novice technologists, and persons who were skilled technologists but novice genealogists.

In recent times, the Information Highway came through and the two disciplines met. Still, most resources for the combined activities have been aimed at either one or both of these groups. Now a third group is appearing: people who are novices in both disciplines but have both interests. For those people, a general resource to explain both areas is a very useful tool. The most recent entry in the *Sams Teach Yourself Today* series hits the target dead center. Terri Stephens Lamb has produced an ideal resource for people who are new to genealogy and to technology, but want to learn more about both.

The book is a quick read, with well-focused chapters aimed at specific topics. The manner is straightforward without a lot of technobabble. I liked two features: the workshops and the quizzes. Each chapter has a "Workshop" section that resembles an FAQ for that topic. At the end of each chapter, the nerds in the audience will take special pleasure from the short quizzes. Others will be relieved to find the answers right after the questions.

Although its stated use is to teach yourself, this book would be an ideal text for a beginner-level class in e-Genealogy, which is the use of technology in genealogy. If you're already familiar with one or the other, *Sams Teach Yourself e-Genealogy Today* is a good way to improve the other skill, and should remain on your reference shelf for a long time.

Beau Sharbrough, President

GENTECH (*www.gentech.org*)

Acknowledgments

How can I possibly say thank you properly to all those who were so inspirational, supportive, and helpful during this project? The truth is, I don't know how. But please bear with me while I try.

First, I want to thank my family for instilling in me the love of history and the desire to never stop learning. My husband deserves a special mention for knowing me so well and loving me anyway. I couldn't have done this without his belief in me.

Many thanks go to all the folks involved in the development and production of this book. Jeff Schultz and Ned Snell have my special thanks for neither talking down to me nor treating me with kid gloves, and for finding me whenever I felt a bit lost.

Much love and gratitude goes to the many folks I've encountered online and with whom I formed real-world friendships over the past few years. You are my extended family, and you know who you are (if I tried to thank you by name, I'd probably make a mess of it).

And finally, a hundred million more thanks are due to people I've never met. They are the generous folks who were pioneers in the field of online genealogy, and those who continue to share their knowledge and their families with the rest of us.

INTRODUCTION

Dear Reader...

Aha, I caught you peeking! That's a good thing, actually. Now I have the opportunity to welcome you to my world—the world of e-Genealogy, that is.

I do other things besides research my family history, but this is a hobby that never quits. Have I ever been frustrated? Yes. Have I experienced delays and setbacks? Of course. Have I ever suffered a loss of my work? Sure did. But I haven't stopped—after all, as long as babies continue to be born, a family tree is never finished!

The joy of learning about my ancestors is just too great to let adversity cause me to give up this never-ending quest. And since you're reading at least this portion of the book, I must assume that you, too, are interested in tracing your family history. Or maybe someone misunderstood when you said *geology*, and you received this as a gift. (Did I see a smile?)

In any case, let me tell you more about it so you can decide whether this book is right for you, or whether to use its pages for a bird cage liner. (Okay, you can stop giggling now.) You can make your way down the e-Genealogy path as quickly or as slowly as you like. I'll be right beside you; that's me holding the flashlight.

What This Book Is

You're probably fairly new to genealogy in general, or maybe you're a more experienced genealogist who is just now beginning to check out Internet resources. In any case, my focus will be about how to research online, so I'm assuming you already have a computer and are already connected to the Net (well, maybe not at this very moment). I'm also assuming that you're not totally new to computers and that you have at least some (however minimal) experience with navigating the Internet.

I'll be covering some of the basic stuff a genealogical newbie will need to know, and I'll also let you in on extra tips and hints I've personally learned. The book is structured as an informal tutorial, and you'll find plenty of opportunities to practice what you learn at your own personal pace. I'll be telling you of the kinds of resources you can expect to find online (and some ways to use them), and you'll learn to find even more yourself.

Instead of telling you what you *can't* do on the Net, I'll be telling you what you *can* do. You may feel a bit overwhelmed by all the information available online, but you'll soon learn how to gain control and make the Internet work for you.

What This Book Isn't

This isn't intended to be a comprehensive instruction book for traditional genealogy research in addition to using the Net. I will be mentioning some offline resources, but not in great detail. If you're a total newbie to genealogy, you'll certainly learn enough here to make a great start. But if your goal is to become an expert in genealogy, you might also want to consider purchasing a book about general research methodology as a companion to this one.

This book also won't cover every tiny detail of online research. My philosophy is like the saying, "Give a family some fish and you'll feed them for a day; teach them to fish and you'll feed them for a lifetime." If I tried to point to where every item is located, I'd be feeding you for a day. But when you learn what's out there, how to find it, and how to use it, you'll be fed for a lifetime. If you were looking for a genealogical Web site directory, you'll probably want another book.

Although we'll discuss genealogy software occasionally, I won't be reviewing or recommending specific programs. Realistically speaking, there is no "best" software title, anyway. Your choice should depend on your particular needs and preferences. You'll find a list of software sites in Appendix A, "Recommended Sites," and you'll learn to find software reviews online.

Ready, Set, Go!

If you're not a beginner to genealogy in general, but you are new to online research, you can skip from right here to Chapter 2, "Getting Started," in which you'll learn how to get going with e-Genealogy. If you already know the basics of online genealogy research, skip ahead to Chapter 3, "Who, Where, and When?," in which you'll learn new skills or refine older ones. However, Chapters 1 and 2 are worth at least a quick look because you never know what you might learn along the way.

I wish you generous helpings of serendipity as you begin—or continue—your adventure. If something you learn here helps you find an ancestor (or if you just want to say hello), feel free to send me an email. Happy rooting!

Terri Stephens Lamb

tegger@ancestry.com

PART I

Laying the Groundwork

CHAPTER 1

First Things First

If you're like most people interested in genealogy, you can hardly wait to jump in with both hands and feet to get your family tree growing. After all, the Internet has made so much more information available than ever before (sometimes within reach by just a few mouse clicks). However, a bit of preparation now can help prevent hours of frustration later, as well as reams of wasted paper and countless episodes of needlessly strained eyes. Like all things worth doing, your family tree is worth doing well. Luckily, you can save many hours of trial-and-error by learning from the mistakes of others—some of them mine—as well as by learning tips for successful research.

Can you find any genealogical information you desire on the Internet? No, not yet. That is, unless your desires are relatively narrow or you're extraordinarily lucky. Though we're all fortunate to enjoy large amounts of available data online, there is still much more that isn't online yet. Eventually, we may not need to rely on more traditional research resources, but for now you might want to consider online resources a companion to offline resources.

This book will focus on *e-Genealogy* (electronic genealogy, or online research) because there are already many excellent sources to help you learn more traditional methods. By using this book, you'll learn what you *can* do online and you'll be ahead of the game by using the Internet to its fullest potential as it continues to grow and evolve.

What You'll Learn in This Chapter:

▶ That your reason for wanting to trace your family history can influence your research methods.

▶ Which research style is right for you.

▶ Why you must begin with what you already know and always work backward through generations.

▶ Some common beginner mistakes and how to avoid them.

By the Way

If you're not a beginner to genealogy in general but are new to online research, you can skip to Chapter 2, "Getting Started," in which you'll learn how to begin with e-Genealogy. However, Chapter 1 is worth at least a quick look because you never know what you might learn along the way.

Your Motivation and Goals

There are probably as many reasons for undertaking genealogy as there are people who do so. There is no such thing as a right answer or a wrong one—it's entirely a matter of personal preference and choice. However, actually naming your motivation(s) will help define your goal(s), which will in turn help determine research and presentation methods that will work best for you.

What's Your Reason?

Go ahead, think it over. Don't rush, and don't worry about getting a "wrong answer" because there are none. In fact, you won't even be quizzed on this. You might want to write down your thoughts as you go—or type them into your favorite word processor—to help guide your focus toward your ultimate goal.

One man was so curious about why folks do genealogy that he decided to ask several thousand fellow family historians. Bill Merklee asked the question, "Why do you do genealogy?" in the ROOTS-L email discussion group. Mr. Merklee was kind enough to present many of his interesting replies (see the following figure); you might find that someone else shares your own reasons.

Sharing perspectives: Many reasons are given for undertaking genealogy.

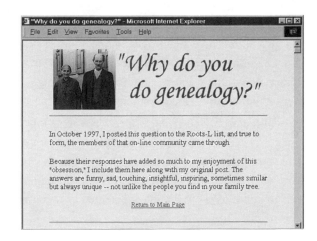

Try It Yourself ▼

1. Connect to the Internet and open your Web browser.

2. Type *www.netrom.com/~merklee/why.html* into your browser's address or location bar, then press Enter.

3. Read Bill Merklee's introduction, then scroll down to read his original ROOTS-L post and its subsequent replies.

▲

Continuing Work Begun by Others

Maybe your Great Aunt Millie was your family's historian until her eyesight failed some time around the end of World War II, and no one has kept up the research since then. You want to pick up the trail before it goes completely cold. Or maybe jolly old Uncle Harry has been the family genealogist for the past 50 years, but you see too many possible errors and would like to verify his work (and continue even farther) because Harry is about to retire from researching.

Medical History

Perhaps you or someone else in your family has symptoms of an illness that may be a congenital disorder. You'd like to compile a medical family history to help with diagnosis and treatment. Or maybe you want to identify possible inherited medical problems to prevent them from becoming serious illnesses.

Snobby Hobby?

Contrary to old-fashioned thinking, most genealogists are not snooty blue-bloods; most possess humor and generosity in equal measure.

Religious Reasons

Maybe you're a member of the Church of Jesus Christ of Latter-Day Saints or another religious denomination or order in which family history is a sacred matter. This might be one of the most personal reasons for tracing a family history, and if this is yours, I'm sure you've already spent time in deep consideration.

Famous Ancestors

Thinking of those exciting family legends? Well, that's okay. But be sure to start with yourself and work backward in order to find out for sure if that famous person is your ancestor! (See "Be Wary of Family Legends" later in this chapter.) Just don't be too disappointed if you find that your ancestor was a small-time thief instead of an industrial tycoon. Sometimes the not-so-famous ancestors are more fun, anyway, and there's even a site to honor your "black sheep" ancestors (see the following figure).

*The Black Sheep
Society honors
your dastardly
ancestors.*

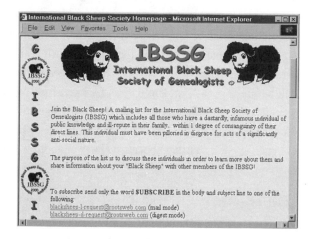

Maybe you already found certain evidence that shows you might
be eligible for membership in a heritage society, such as the
Daughters of the American Revolution (D.A.R.) or a similar organization. Because these types of organizations generally require
verifiable proof of heritage, you'll want to find that proof in order
to become a member.

Curiosity About Heritage

Has someone teased you about your Irish temperament? your
Gallic tastes in food? your Oriental sense of economy? your
Native American looks? Yet all these years you thought your fam-
ily was originally from Germany on your father's side and from
Italy on your mother's side.

Perhaps you're an adoptee searching for your birth family. Maybe
you're an African-American who wonders if your ancestors were
slaves. Possibly you're the only person with blue eyes in your
immediate family, and you want to know where you got them. Or
maybe you simply feel some need that you can't quite define.

Whatever your reasons, you're curious and would like to know
who your ancestors were, where they might have come from, how
they lived, and how different or similar to yourself they might
have been.

What Do You Want to Accomplish?

Now that you've identified your reasons for undertaking the task
of tracing your family history, it's time to decide what you want

to achieve. Let's look at some common goals, but keep in mind that any one goal is not necessarily exclusive to any other, and this is by no means an exhaustive set of ideas to explore. Genealogy often becomes a lifelong endeavor, and you'll likely eventually set and achieve many different goals. But you have to start somewhere!

Family Trees and Charts

A family tree chart might be one of the easiest and quickest goals to achieve. It can be large or small, formal or fanciful, simple or detailed. Your reasons for constructing the chart will determine how simple or complex it should be.

The following figure shows an example of a decorative wall chart you can purchase or create from scratch.

The Genie Bug

Family history enthusiasts often laughingly refer to themselves as having been bitten by the genealogy bug—it's an addictive hobby!

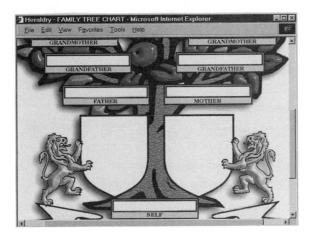

An example of a simple family tree wall chart.

The next figure shows just one of the many charts you might be able to create with your genealogy software.

Maybe you'd like to include the kids in a fun family project by enlisting them to help you construct a family tree wall chart for your den. Any number of materials could be used to decorate the chart, and depending on the amount of detail, this might even be a project your kids could do on their own. You might only need to do a minimal amount of research for a simple project like this, but do be sure to keep organized notes in case you want to dig deeper later on.

A portion of a family tree chart you might make with software such as The Master Genealogist.

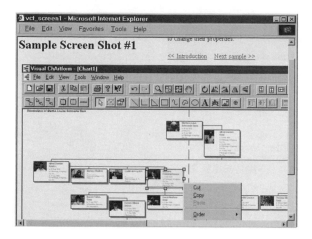

If your chart will be based on medical conditions or verifiable proof of ancestry, attention to detail is especially important both in researching and constructing the chart. The same is true if you want a formal pedigree chart, which is similar to a family tree chart, but it usually only follows a single line of male direct descendents.

Story and Biography Collections

This is another goal that may be anywhere between fairly simple and quite detailed, and either formal or informal. These collections might go hand-in-hand with another goal—as a companion to a family tree chart or included as part of a family history book.

Stories may be compiled from oral and/or written histories of people, places, and events meaningful to your family. Though informal story collections needn't be verified for total accuracy, do include annotations, and make an effort to provide as much factual information as possible (that is, don't include a known fabrication just because it sounds good unless you add explanatory notes). Some genealogists like to include favorite family recipes, holiday traditions, or jokes in such collections.

Formalized family stories and biographies should be as accurate as possible, but that doesn't mean they can't be fun and fulfilling to compile. Again, be sure your readers can tell the difference between fact and family folklore.

Family History Books

Though it might sound somewhat daunting, writing a family history book has never been easier. You can't do it without researching first, but many current genealogy software products include the ability to compile a book almost automatically by using the data you add as you progress. You might or might not be pleased with the resulting book in its rawest form, but you can always add more details and formatting later, and such software can help make your task easier.

The following figure shows a sample page from a book that might be created with genealogy software (this example is for the ancestors of John F. Kennedy).

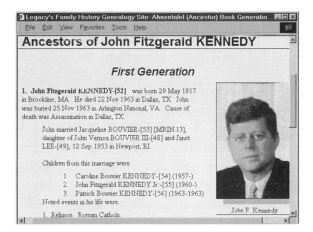

Gathering Stories

Family reunions and other gatherings are great places to get older relatives to tell their stories. Record them on paper or on tape!

A family history book you might make with software such as Legacy Family Tree.

Databases to Share

Maybe you're the designated genealogist for your family, but you don't necessarily want to be responsible for compiling a book or making family tree charts. If you like, you can collect data to share with your family so they can do their own family history projects. This takes dedication and a generous spirit because you'll work hard with little reward beyond personal satisfaction in the sense of achievement you'll feel. Attention to detail and constant verification are at the top of your list. Sometimes you'll feel frustrated enough to quit, but you'll keep going because the genealogy bug has bitten you!

Research Styles

Now that you've decided what you want to do and why you want to do it, it's time to look at some methods you might use to achieve your goals.

Formal Genealogies

Accuracy and attention to detail are constant requirements if you want to present your family history in a formalized manner. You need a structured research plan, excellent organization, loads of patience, a good deal of time, and an active sense of humor to travel this route. Your research plan will include setting strict goals, achieving goals by poring through minute details, keeping accurate notes and source citations, and staying organized.

This approach might sound boring to some, but it doesn't have to be. Even if some tasks do become tedious at times, your diligence will be rewarded with well-researched project results.

A More Homespun Approach

Although constant verification of data isn't as important with an informal approach to family history as it is with a more formal genealogy project, it *is* important to be as accurate as possible. Your research plan can be somewhat less structured, but you shouldn't include data or information based merely on hearsay, rumor, or family legend alone. Be fair to fellow researchers when sharing your work—if any of your information is unverified, even if based on good evidence, *say so*.

Begin with Yourself

A Family Bush?

Don't worry if your family tree more closely resembles a bush. Even the mightiest oak tree was once very small.

The number one mistake made by many beginners in genealogy is trying to start with a person they believe to be their family's earliest ancestor. At first, that might seem a reasonable place to start, but it's actually a route destined to confuse and frustrate you before you get very far (unless you're extremely lucky, that is).

Think of a family tree as growing from the ground up, with yourself represented by the trunk of the tree and your parents and other ancestors represented by branches, limbs, twigs, and leaves, each growing progressively smaller toward the top. Just as a tree branches out, so should your research (see the following figure).

If you were to begin with a person several generations back, you would need to research every child of that early ancestor. Next, you would research each of those children's spouses, and each of *their* children's spouses and children, and so on down the line in a circuitous and tiresome path. Eventually you'd find whether that path leads to yourself. It might not lead to you at all, and you would have wasted considerable time you could have used to research people who actually *were* your ancestors.

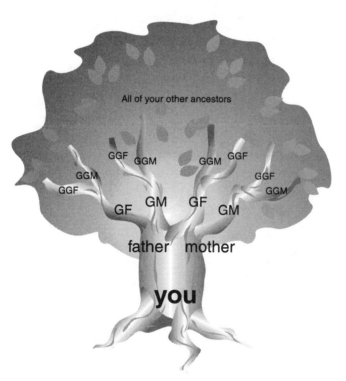

Notice that you are at the base of the tree.

Be Wary of Family Legends

Many families have at least one story that tells of being related to someone famous (for example, a royal personage or president, an actor, an author, a musician, an outlaw, a scientist, a war hero). Some of the stories may turn out to be true, and many do contain at least a grain of truth. Hearing stories of famous ancestors is tempting, but *never* begin your research by trying to follow a famous person's line of descent to your own family. For the same reasons mentioned earlier, begin with yourself and work your way back through the ancestors you encounter. Eventually you'll prove whether or not your family is actually related to the person in your family's legend.

Even if you don't know of any famous folks in your family, never assume that just because certain tales have been told for generations that they must be true. Sometimes they will turn out to be true, but more often the passage of time has distorted many of the facts.

The following figure shows one famous historical figure that many might have fun claiming as their own, but the truth is that Dracula has very few living descendants.

Vlad Tepes (a.k.a. Vlad Dracula), a whole different meaning for "blood ancestor"?

Basic Conventions and Customs Used in Genealogy

Like folks involved in other hobbies, genealogists sometimes seem to have a language of their own. Luckily, it isn't difficult to learn and there are relatively few rules written in stone, but your research will go more smoothly if you learn a few standard ways of doing certain things.

Names, Dates, and Locations

You'll learn more details later in the book, but this section shows some basic, commonly accepted styles of recording most American and many European-style names, dates, and locations.

Names

Most names should be recorded in the following style: First name, ("Nickname"), Middle name, (Maiden Surname [for married females]), SURNAME, and title abbreviation, if any. All names should be spelled entirely except when only an initial is known or the name is completely unknown. Unknown first and/or middle names may be indicated with a question mark, but unknown surnames should be designated as "UNKNOWN." Names known to be non-existent (such as nicknames or middle names) may be omitted.

Examples for recording names:

Bernard ("B.L.") Lee STEPHENS, Rev.
Verdell (Hickey) STEPHENS
Eldred Arnold PERRY
Bernice Pearly (Donaldson) PERRY
John Dison BALL, Jr.
Nancy (Brown) BALL
James ("Jim") Samuel GRIGGS
Beulah Delilah (Sheppard) GRIGGS
James H. LAMB
Nora (Lyons) LAMB
James ("Jim") MCCLURE
Mrs. ? (Unknown) MCCLURE

Dates

Dates in genealogical records are almost always recorded in a day, month, and year format as follows: *dd mon year* (for example, 28 Aug 1999 or 01 Jan 1801). This style is used as a standard to avoid confusion because of the variety of date styles used around the world. Most genealogists use a variation of this style, but be aware that many records exist with other date styles, so be sure to check before recording them. For example, suppose you find a birth record dated 3/1/12. You'll need to know the dating method for that record before you know which set of digits represents the day, the month, and the year. You'll probably find that the date translates to either 3 Jan 1912 or 1 Mar 1912, but be careful in case it actually means something else—maybe an earlier century.

Did You Notice?

Surnames are always shown in ALL CAPS except for the maiden surnames of married women. This helps researchers identify surnames quickly when sifting through data.

Locations

This book focuses on North American research, but you may
want to share your findings with folks from around the world.
Keep in mind that not everyone is familiar with U.S. or Canadian
geo-political structure or associated abbreviations, so it's a good
idea to get in the habit of spelling out exactly what you mean.
The most commonly accepted format for recording North
American locations is *City, County* (or *Parish* or *Borough), State*
(or *Province)*.

For example, I would record my residence in 1999 as
Chattanooga, Hamilton County, Tennessee. Some genealogists
might abbreviate the city name, change *County* to *Co.* or omit the
word entirely, and/or abbreviate the state name (as in Chatta.,
Hamilton, Tenn.). However, that can become confusing, especially when you record a city that shares a name with its county.
Many people would likely have no idea what *Chatta.* means, and
some might not know what *Tenn.* means, either. That's why it's
better to spell out the place names.

In any case, always include the three basic elements of a location,
and if you simply must use abbreviations, try to limit them to the
County and State names, using standard postal codes (in this case,
it would look like Chattanooga, Hamilton Co., TN). That way, it
would be easier for someone unfamiliar with the abbreviations to
find their meaning.

Common Abbreviations

The most common abbreviations you'll see in genealogical
research are *b.* (*born* or *birth*), *m.* (*married* or *marriage*), and *d.*
(*died* or *death*). Those are fairly self-explanatory, but there are a
few others you'll also need to know:

> *abt.—About,* as in "Joe Smith b. abt. 1899."
>
> *aft.—After,* as in "Joe Smith b. aft. 1898."
>
> *bef.—Before,* as in "Joe Smith b. bef. 1900."
>
> *bet.—Between,* as in "Joe Smith b. bet. 1898–1900."
>
> *fr.—From,* as in "Joe Smith in school fr. 1906–1914."

Common Terms

As you research, you'll come across a variety of genealogical terms, abbreviations, and acronyms you may not be familiar with. Many of these will be explained as you progress through this book, and many more can be found in the "Glossary" section.

In addition, you'll find much more information online, such as the relationship chart shown in the following figure.

Sorting out those confusing family relationships is made easier by online help.

The Bottom Line

Congratulations! You're on your way. In addition to some possible surprises you might have learned in this chapter, you should know

- That your reasons for undertaking e-Genealogy as a hobby can help you decide on your first goal.

- That your goal affects your research methodology.

- Some basic knowledge to help prevent common mistakes along the way.

Workshop

Use the following workshop to help reinforce the knowledge you've gained in this lesson.

What's That Word?

In addition to using this book's Glossary, you can find many sites online to help define terms that are new to you.

Q Can I find my Irish great-great-grandfather online?

A If you do, he'd be in remarkable health for such an elderly
man! Seriously, it depends. You might find data for him on a
Web site or in an email discussion group, or maybe his information isn't yet available online. In any case, don't get ahead
of yourself—begin with *you* and work backward through the
generations.

**Q Can I compile a family history by using the stories my
grandmother told me?**

A Yes, you can use those stories as clues and extra colorful
details. But if you want your family history to be accurate,
you'll need to research and verify all names, dates, and
events.

**Q I don't know if I want to spend years researching my
family. Is it worth even starting?**

A Yes, it's well worth your time, even if you don't decide to
continue the quest. Whatever information you find will benefit others in your family who may be interested. Besides, you
might be bitten by the genealogy bug along the way. This is
an affectionate term that means what begins as a hobby turns
into an avocation for many people.

Quiz

Take the following quiz to see how much you've learned.

Questions

1. True or False: You can find almost any information you seek
   on the Internet.

2. Translate the following: John Maxwell BROWN b. 18 Oct
   1888, m. Elizabeth JOHNSON bef. 1910, d. abt. 1918.

3. True or False: You should get in the habit of recording dates
   in the format of day, month, and year, as in 13 Jun 1980.

4. True or False: You shouldn't even bother tracing your family
   tree unless you have lots of money and many years to spend.

Answers

1. False. You can't find everything online yet, but it's getting there!

2. John Maxwell BROWN was born on the 18th of October, 1888, he married Elizabeth JOHNSON sometime before 1910, and he died about 1918.

3. True. Standardized dating conventions will help genealogists worldwide share data without confusion.

4. False. You can undertake genealogical research with minimal expenses by using modern technology, and results are often much quicker than they were with traditional methods.

CHAPTER 2

Getting Started

Growing a family tree is sometimes compared to actual gardening. Like a gardener, you'll plant your tree and tend it in hopes of enjoying its fruits as it matures. Also like a gardener, you'll need some basic tools to get started, and you may add other tools for more specialized purposes either now or later. But unlike gardening tools, e-Genealogy tools don't have to be hosed off at the end of the day!

Consider your computer system the foundation on which your collection of tools will be built—perhaps you might think of an electronic gardening shed. In this chapter, you'll learn which e-Genealogy tools you shouldn't be without plus some extra ones that can help make your tasks even more fun and efficient. You'll also take a "crash course" in searching the Internet to learn the basic skills you'll need to help you find what you seek.

Hardware, Software, and More

You don't need the newest and fastest computer system available and lots of fancy software and peripheral equipment to be successful with e-Genealogy. You'll find it harder to get by with a dinosaur of a machine, though. In this section you'll learn what you *must have*, what you *should have*, and what you *might want* to help make your project go smoother.

Minimum System Requirements

Table 2.1 shows a list of the minimum system requirements you'll need for a truly successful foray into the world of online genealogical research, along with a list of preferred requirements. You might get by with older or less powerful hardware, an earlier operating system, and/or older additional software, but keep in mind that it's difficult to find new software for them, and few

What You'll Learn in This Chapter:

▶ The minimum equipment and software requirements you'll need for successful research.

▶ Some tools for organization.

▶ How to keep track of what's what.

▶ Tips on using search engines effectively.

By the Way

If you already know the basics of online genealogy research, you can skip to the next chapter. There you'll learn more skills and improve upon those you've already learned.

older software titles are still supported. Also be aware that newer software titles usually have their own minimum requirements, and some of those might require even more than what I've listed. Most likely you'll find that you already have at least the minimum requirements listed, and you may have even more.

Table 2.1   Minimum and Preferred System Requirements

Item	Minimum	Preferred
Processor	100MHz	266MHz or higher Pentium or equivalent
Hard drive free space	500MB	1GB or more
RAM	8MB	32MB or more
Modem	14.4Kbps	28.8Kbps or faster
Operating system	Windows 95, Mac OS 7.5, or other equivalent	Most recent version
Web/email	Ver. 3.01 Netscape or MSIE/Outlook Express	Most recent versions
ISP/online service	Your preference	Your preference

Tools for Organization

Fine Print?

You probably don't absolutely need a printer, but I don't know what I'd do without mine!

Table 2.2 shows a list of the minimum tools you'll need to organize and maintain your research, along with a list of preferred requirements. You'll notice that you probably already have at least the minimum requirements.

Table 2.2   Minimum and Preferred Organizational Tools

Purpose	Minimum	Preferred
Group sheets	Word processor, printer	Genealogy software, printer
Research logs, notes	Word processor, printer	Genealogy software, printer
Other forms	Word processor, printer	Custom forms on your hard drive, printer
Master database	Database/spreadsheet software, printer	Genealogy software, printer
Physical documents	None	Folders and/or notebooks

Extra Tools for Fun and Effectiveness

Table 2.3 shows some extra tools you might want to use to further enhance your research experience and your eventual project presentations. These aren't absolutely necessary for fun and effective research and results, but you might want to consider using them. You probably already have at least some of these extras, but it's completely up to you to decide whether and in what ways you want to use them or to purchase new equipment or software for your e-Genealogy projects.

Table 2.3   Minimum and Suggested Extra Tools

Item	Minimum	Suggested
Scanner	Small handheld	Flatbed, legal size documents or larger
CD-ROM	2x speed	8x or faster
Sound card	8-bit	16-bit or better
Graphics software	Basic picture viewer	Multi-format graphics viewer/editor
Search software	Hard drive file searcher	Hard drive and Internet searcher
Backups	Lots of 3.5" disks	Internal or external backup drive
Desktop publishing software	Word processor, graphics software, printer	Software that meets your needs, printer
Web site software	Text editor	HTML editor, FTP software

You can read actual user reviews of a variety of titles on the Genealogy Software SpringBoard at *www.gensoftsb.com* (shown in the following figure).

Where's the Wares?

See the "Software" section of Appendix A, "Recommended Sites." There you'll find a list of popular genealogy software titles.

*Real people
review genealogy
software and
utilities.*

```
Genealogy Software Springboard - Home Page - Microsoft Internet Explorer  _ □ ×
 File   Edit   View   Favorites   Tools   Help

 WINDOWS
 SOFTWARE                    Genealogy Software SpringBoard
 Ancestors & Descendants
 Ancestral Quest
 Behold (under development)       Last Update: September 01, 1999 11:32 AM
 NEW  BirthWrite                Visitor #  161985  since May 8, 1996
 Brothers Keeper
 Create Family Trees
 Cumberland Family Tree
 Dynas Tree
 Family Explorer            GENERAL GENEALOGY SOFTWARE SURVEY 1 - Click on t
 Family Matters                    VoteBot Button for Survey Results
 Family Origins
 Family Reunion               ×  Genealogy Software Springboard - General Software Survey 1
 Family Treasures
 Family Tree Maker         Started: 02 Aug 1999 05:03 GMT, Duration: 4 weeks, Ended: 30 Aug 19
 Fzip Family Tree                             05:03 GMT
 GenDesigner
 GeneWeb
 Generations Family Tree
 NEW  Generations -
 Family Tree Builder            GenSoftSB - OUR MISSION
 NEW  Genesis            This site was created in 1996 in order to help our fellow rooters
 Genius Family Tree      genealogists review genealogy programs. Since then, thousands
 GenTree97
```

Try It Yourself ▼

▼

1. Connect to the Internet and open your Web browser.

2. Type *www.gensoftsb.com* into your browser's address or location bar and press Enter. Once there, click on the Selecting Software link (upper-left side of your screen).

3. Read the brief advice on how to select software that meets your needs, then look around at the different software titles reviewed on the site.

▲

Getting Organized

Now that you've learned the basic tools you'll need, it's time to start using them to get organized. Individuals vary widely in organizational skills and preferences, so consider these suggestions as basic guidelines. Regardless of your actual style, it pays to know what's what and where it is. Although my desk would appear messy and cluttered to most people, there is a method to the madness. (Or so I tell myself!)

Avoid Confusion from the Start

When it comes to avoiding confusion, this is one definite case of "Do as I say, not as I do" (or as I did, I should say). I learned the hard way—finding myself in a state of complete befuddlement—to organize my research materials. I'm still not the greatest organizer in the world, but at least I'm not constantly confused now. Well, not about e-Genealogy, anyway.

Review the notes you made when deciding your research goals to help you stay focused. You may want to take extra notes as we look at the tools you'll need to help fine-tune your research plan (after all, that's part of getting organized). In this section you'll learn more details about the tools you saw listed in Table 2.2.

Family Group Sheets

Family group sheets can be found in styles from fairly simple to quite detailed, but you're going to need them in one style or another. You can obtain blank hard copies to fill in by hand from LDS Family History Centers and other genealogy organizations. Alternately, you can realize your computer's potential by making them yourself (and you'll save a trip at the same time). You can make your own by using your word processor, but your task will be even simpler if you use genealogy software that allows you to print blank forms or group sheets using the data you input. An additional option is to find blank forms online to print from your Web browser.

Ideally, you should make a family group sheet for each individual you research, so you'll need lots of these forms. The basic components of each group sheet include

Main individual's full name

Individual's father and mother

Date and place of birth

Date and place of marriage

Date and place of death

Individual's spouse's full name

Spouse's father and mother

Spouse's date and place of birth

Spouse's date and place of death

Child #1's gender and full name

Child #1's spouse's name

Child #1's date and place of birth

Child #1's date and place of marriage

Child #1's date and place of death

Similar data for all other children

Designated area for brief notes

Extra components might include areas to record other marriages, jobs, military career, religion, residences, physical descriptions, or other information pertinent to the main individual.

The next two figures show examples of different styles of family group sheets you might come across on the Web.

A simple family group sheet...

...and a slightly fancier one in Web table format.

Wedding Train Spotting

If an individual was married more than once, be sure to record children from a particular marriage on the properly corresponding group sheet (instead of recording all the children born to an individual on one sheet). Otherwise, you're bound to become confused and maybe stay that way!

Research Logs and Notes

You'll need research logs to keep track of who and what you've researched plus when, where, and how you checked for information. You'll also want to keep notes on what you found, what you didn't find, and possible leads to research later. Logs can be in a free-form style, and you can write them on paper or type them into your word processor. However, most researchers find that it helps to settle on a standardized form to help them remember what they've done and what they plan to do in the future. You can use printed hard copies of such forms, or you can make your own using your word processor or genealogy software. You can also find these forms online to print from your Web browser.

Other Forms

You'll probably want to use other forms to record certain data, such as census records. Again, you can obtain hard copies of such forms, make your own, or you can get them from the Web.

Master Database

It doesn't matter whether it's a simple list of names, dates, locations, and other details for the individuals you've researched or a genealogy software package chock full of your data. You need some sort of master database to bring your research together in one place. Regardless of your methods, don't wait too long before starting on your database; begin compiling it along with your first family group sheets and maintain it regularly as you research. This task is usually automated if you use one of the currently popular genealogy database software titles, such as the one shown in the following figure.

Free Form Help

You'll find a variety of resources for obtaining different kinds of online forms and other aids at *genealogy.about.com*.

Physical Documents

You'll likely accumulate quite a stack of physical documents the
longer you research and as you spend more attention on details.
You may already have photographs in various locations around
your home. You may already have old letters or other keepsakes
that you always meant to organize but never got around to doing.
As you further your research, you may collect copies of birth and
death certificates, marriage licenses, deeds and other land records,
wills and probate records, obituaries and other newspaper or magazine clippings, audio or video recordings, research notes, or
other documents.

Each document represents some event, large or small, in each
ancestor's life. If you keep waiting for "some day" before getting
around to organizing those documents, you might find yourself
swimming in a sea of paper! Most researchers like to keep special
notebooks or folders for their documents, but do organize them in
some way, even if you only use labeled boxes to store them.

Important Stuff!

Be sure to protect your irreplaceable documents and mementos! Make
extra copies of the ones you deem most important and store them
somewhere away from your residence (perhaps with a relative). That
way, if your home suffers damage from a fire, natural disaster, or an act
of malicious mischief, chances are much better that your important
papers will survive.

Citing Sources and Keeping Track

Imagine this scenario: You're on a short trip to a place you've never been before. Suddenly you see a landmark you recognize and you remember that you have indeed visited here before. Now you feel your current trip is a waste of time (and maybe money, too). After all, you could have gone somewhere else if only you had remembered sooner.

How Others Do It

See how some researchers organize their genealogical materials at *www.rootsweb.com/ ~ote/organize.htm.*

Does the scenario sound familiar? If you neglect to cite your sources and keep track of where you've already researched, you'll feel that way every time you find yourself looking for information where you've already looked—especially if your previous attempt was unsuccessful. Consider source citations and research notes the landmarks by which to recognize that you've "visited here before."

Citing Sources Correctly

If you find information in a certain magazine or newspaper, will recording only the name of the publication be enough to help you remember exactly what you found and where you found it? No matter how good your memory may be, it's unlikely you'll remember those details with the passage of time, especially after you've encountered several similar sources. Why might you need to remember those details? Because you may find the need to check again later for missed information or further leads, or to verify clues found elsewhere.

Your source citations should include as many details as you can think of (publication name, date, issue number, article title, article author, page numbers, and so on). This is also true for citing books, Web sites, emails, or any other media as your source for any particular information. Record anything you can to help you remember where you found a certain piece of information. Besides knowing where to go to review information (or to avoid a source that yielded nothing), you'll also have the satisfaction of being able to verify where each piece of the greater puzzle was found.

Suppose you find information on a Web site called "My Family Tree" (a large number of people actually use this as a title for genealogy sites). Certainly the title isn't enough to use for your citation, even if the title of a real site is more memorable. Even including the Web address isn't enough on its own. The Web constantly changes, and some people change their Web sites as often as they change socks. Look for the author or Webmaster's name and email address and send them a brief note. This accomplishes at least two things—you'll display good manners by thanking the person for providing information or help, and at the same time you'll verify that the email address is current.

A Net Peeve

I wish more genealogy Webmasters would title their sites descriptively ("Smith Ancestors" describes more than "Our Ancestors").

Another possibility is that the other person may have more information to share, or you may have information they need. This could be the beginning of a new lifetime relationship that offers the satisfaction of sharing future findings. While you're at a Web site on which you find information, be sure to also check any sources listed at the site. Even if you aren't working on a formalized and absolutely accurate genealogy project, it's always a good idea to double-check your information whenever possible.

The following figure shows a small excerpt from the *Columbia Guide to Online Style*, which explains precise source citation methods for electronic media. We'll discuss this in more detail in Chapter 7, "When You Find Information, Then What?"

The Internet is the best place to learn more about (you guessed it) the Internet.

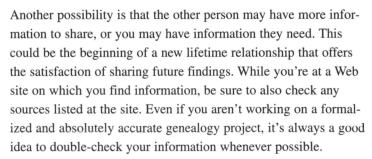
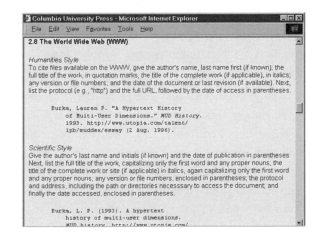

Keeping Track of Where You've Been

Use your research log to record what you were looking for and when, whether you found it, and add notes for any details you

want to include. Some researchers use their Web browser's bookmark function to make quick notes about sites they visit. Then
they collect the notes into their main database at the end of that
session. This is a great idea, but you must remember to back up
your bookmark file often (in case your Web browser crashes) and
remember to collect the notes after you surf.

Internet Searching 101

Searching the Internet for specific information can sometimes
seem like trying to find the proverbial needle in a haystack. You
know it's there, but where? And how do you find it without over-
turning the entire haystack? There's always the possibility that
you might get lucky while surfing Web sites at random, but it's
much more productive to use the help of one or more of the many
search engines available.

Using Search Engines Effectively

Search engines are like physical machines in many ways: they're
hard to break, they can make certain tasks easier, and they can
often be fun to work with. But as smart as search engines have
become, they still can't think or make decisions, and they aren't
perfect. They need your help in order to help *you* better!

To find out if your line of Johnsons is on the Web, you wouldn't
want to type a generic phrase like *Johnson genealogy* into a
search engine. Oh, you'd get plenty of search results. But you'd
get entirely too many to reasonably comb through, and most of
the results won't have anything to do with your particular
Johnsons (some may have nothing to do with *any* Johnsons or
even genealogy at all). Go ahead and try it for yourself. Go to
www.go.com and once there, type *Johnson genealogy* in the
search field. When I tried it, there were over 800,000 search
results! (See the following figure.) Unless you truly want to look
at every site listed (a huge and time-consuming task), you'll need
more specific search terms.

Flip-Flop Engines

A search engine
might yield few or
no results one day,
and another day you
might get thousands
from the same key-
words.

*878,431 search
results are too
many to look at!*

Search results for : Johnson genealogy - Microsoft Internet Explorer

File   Edit   View   Favorites   Tools   Help

Web search results   1 - 10 of 878,431 results most relevant to **Johnson genealogy**

Next 10 > | Hide summaries | Sort by date | Ungroup results

Johnson Genealogy - Emphasis on Horry and Marion County, South Carolina
Johnson Family **Genealogy**
100% **Date: 12 Aug 1999**, Size 10.5K,
http://www.martygrant.com/gen/johnson-sc.htm
Find similar pages | Translate this page

Mayflower Web Pages
Genealogy and history, including lists of Mayflower passengers, Abraham Lincoln's 1863 Thanksgiving proclamation, and full texts of Pilgrims' writings.
100% **Date: 18 Oct 1997**, Size 14.9K,
http://members.aol.com/calebj/mayflower.html
Find similar pages | Translate this page

Family Tree Maker's Genealogy Site: User Home Pages:
McCaskill/Johnson Genealogy
Randall Lynn McCaskill Vienna, VA rmccask@comm-data.com My **genealogy** information on my real web site This is really just a pointer to my other home ...
100% **Date: 22 Apr 1999**, Size 1.9K,

Search Amazon.com
- JOHNSON GENEALO...
- Buy MP3 Players!
- Save Up to 40%!

- CLICK HERE TO SHOP! -

Buy the book

From Borders.com
- Win a Trip to France!
- Star Wars must-haves!
- Everything Austin Powers!
- Sarah Mclachlan Guitar Giveaway!
- Visit our Gift Center!

General Search Terms and Methods

It's usually better to search for specific information on one person at a time than to try for a whole family. Using the previous example, pick an individual from the Johnson family and search for that person. Suppose the ancestor you choose is Alfred Johnson and you know he came from Georgia. In the search field, type *Alfred Johnson Georgia* (if you know a middle name or initial and the city and county, add those, too). When I tried, I came up with no search results, yet I know that at least one page does exist, because I saw it during the earlier search. Don't be discouraged when you seem to find nothing; try changing the search terms. You may need to add a few more keywords or omit a few, or you may need to change the order of the keywords.

Different search engines react in various ways to certain kinds of input, so be prepared to read the help section for each individual engine (these are often seen as text links like *Search Options* or *How to Search* or even *Help*). This doesn't really take as long as it might seem, and you'll be better prepared to use more search engines more effectively.

Specialized Searches

Some Web sites specialize in helping you search within a certain topic (these are often actually Internet directories or *portal sites* rather than true search engines). These can be a great help to point toward resources within the topic, but don't neglect the more general search engines because many new or small Web sites aren't yet indexed in the topical portals. You might like to try one such portal site at *www.genealogy.com*, shown in the following figure. (You'll probably have no trouble memorizing that URL!)

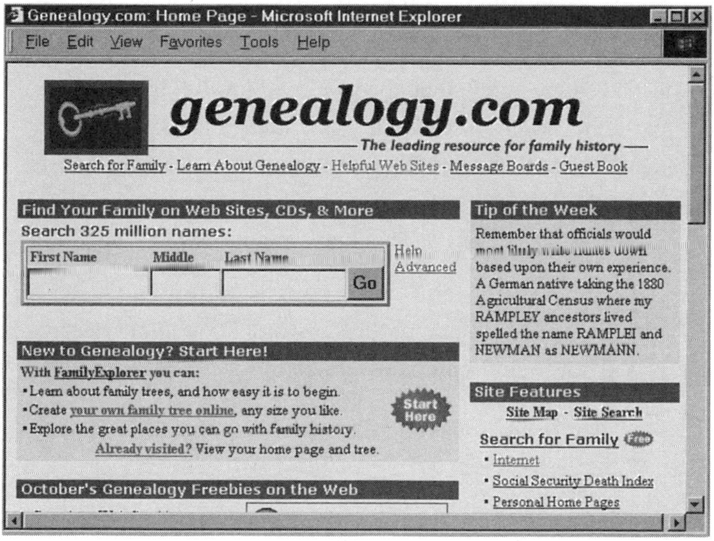

Genealogy.com specializes in (you guessed it) genealogy.

Helpful Tips and Tricks

As you practice, you'll probably pick up more ideas that will help with your individual research situations, but to get you started, you might want to try the following tips and tricks I've personally found helpful:

- Type search terms in all lowercase first, including terms that might normally be capitalized. If that doesn't work well, try search terms as you think they should or might be capitalized.

- Check for typos and spelling errors as you enter search terms.

- Enclose phrases within quotation marks when you want to find an exact phrase on a site.

Did You Know?

All the sites mentioned in this chapter plus many others to help with your e-Genealogy research are listed in Appendix A, "Recommended Sites."

- Use *Boolean expressions* (you can learn more about this in most search engine help sections).

- Search and surf the Web at non-peak hours whenever possible. Online research between 10 p.m. and 8 a.m. Eastern Standard Time usually means faster connections and shorter load times for me because of less Web traffic. This seems to be especially effective for non-U.S. and academic sites (smaller international ISPs and university libraries, for example).

- If you follow a link that appears to be invalid, try deleting part of the URL to see if the main site still exists. (Sometimes Web sites reorganize and change some of their internal URLs, but you can often find the same or similar information as listed in search engine results.)

- If your first search terms don't bring good results, try deliberately misspelling some of the keywords. You might be surprised how helpful this can actually be at times.

More On Searching

Learn all you ever wanted to know (maybe more than you'll ever need) about Web searching at *websearch.about.com*.

Here's a short list of some popular search engines and portal sites:

About.com	*home.about.com*
Alta Vista	*www.altavista.com*
Beaucoup!	*www.beaucoup.com*
BigHub.com	*www.thebighub.com*
Excite	*www.excite.com*
Google!	*www.google.com*
GoTo.com	*www.goto.com*
HotBot	*www.hotbot.com*
LookSmart	*www.looksmart.com*
Lycos Network	*www.lycos.com*
whatUseek	*whatUseek.com*
Yahoo!	*www.yahoo.com*

The Bottom Line

You're on your way to a successful e-Genealogy project. In addition to some possible surprises you might have learned in this chapter, you should know

- Which tools you can't do without and some ways to use them.

- Some extra tools you can use to enhance your online research experience.

- Basic organizational and Internet search skills.

Workshop

Use the following workshop to help reinforce the knowledge you've gained in this lesson.

Q I have a 486 computer with Windows 3.1, 4MB RAM, and a 9600bps modem. Can I be successful in e-Genealogy?

A Yes, but the tools available to you are much more limited and it may take you a good deal longer to get satisfactory results. Though it's certainly possible to be successful, I would definitely recommend upgrading to or purchasing a more current system to fully enjoy the greater potential of the wider range of possibilities.

Q I don't have any genealogy software. Can I still research my family history online?

A Yes. As long as you have the minimum hardware and software requirements for e-Genealogy, using genealogy software isn't absolutely necessary. But I can tell you from experience that using genealogy software that meets your particular needs will make your project much easier.

Q I tried searching for my family by typing "Jones genealogy" into a search engine. Why can't I find them?

A The main reason is most likely because your search term was too broad, especially considering the fact that the family name is so common. Try using more restrictive terms such as individual names, places, dates, and so on.

Quiz

Take the following quiz to see how much you've learned.

Questions

1. True or False: You need the newest and fastest computer system and software to be successful in e-Genealogy.

2. Name some common ways to obtain family group sheets.

3. True or False: A Web site's title and URL are all you need to cite the source when you find information there.

4. True or False: If a search engine returns zero results, you can often find results by changing your search terms.

Answers

1. False. You'll find it more difficult using an outdated machine, but you don't need a "speed demon" either!

2. You can obtain hard copies from offline sources; you can make your own with a word processor and printer; your genealogy software may allow you to print copies; or you can find copies online that you can print.

3. False. The site may eventually change its title and/or its URL, so you need more details if you want to verify or check for more information later.

4. True. Every search engine performs in different ways, so don't be afraid to experiment.

PART II

Finding Your Family Online... Literally

CHAPTER 3

Who, Where, and When?

Though WWW usually means *World Wide Web*, in genealogy the abbreviation could also represent the three most common questions you'll ask as you search: "Who, where, and when?" You'll be dealing most extensively with names, places, and dates in your research, so let's learn more about them first. As you progress, you might want to add "What, why, and how?" to the mix, but we'll get to those later in the book.

In this chapter you'll learn about first names, nicknames, and surnames to help you figure out *who* you're looking for. You'll also learn about using online geographic resources to help find clues for *where* to look (or to locate where your ancestors lived). Then you'll learn more about dates to help find *when* specific events happened. When you've learned these three W's, you'll be ready to advance to more specific e-Genealogy research resources and methods.

What You'll Learn in This Chapter:

▶ A brief history on the origin of surnames.

▶ How first names and middle names can either help or confuse you.

▶ Why maps and other geographic tools are important to genealogists.

▶ The difference between Julian and Gregorian calendars.

Surnames: The Common Denominator

Surnames (family names) aren't necessarily always last. Most American names do present the surname last in order when written or spoken; this is often true even if the name is adapted from an origin in which surnames are presented in a different order. But for the purposes of genealogy research, a surname is usually "first" in the sense that it is most often the first clue by which to find data on a person within a given family.

Surname Basics

In an earlier time, it didn't really matter if your name was simply Donald or Mary. Ancient Romans had used an elaborate three-name system for a few hundred years, but the practice disappeared after the Empire fell. In any case, it was unlikely that anyone near you had the same name. Even if someone in another village happened to share your name, you probably wouldn't have known them because the vast majority of people in those times didn't travel much. As a result, there was no pressing need to differentiate all the Donalds and Marys. However, as the world became more populated and people did travel more, they eventually needed a way to avoid confusion.

By the Way

The best resources for specific surname meanings and origins are in your local library, but you can also find some excellent material online.

Most early surnames were really descriptions based on an occupation, a location, or a personality trait or physical characteristic. You might hear of Donald the Farmer in one village or Donald of the Hill at another. People might speak of Mary the Small at one place and Mary the Gentle somewhere else. Table 3.1 shows a list of some common names and their probable early origins.

Table 3.1   Some Common Surnames and Origins

Occupation	Location	Trait/Characteristic
Brewer	Brook	Armstrong
Carpenter	Dale	Friendly
Mason	Forest or Forrest	Good or Goode
Merchant	Glen	Long
Smith	Lane	Moody
Turner	London or Paris	Stout
Wright	Wood or Woods	Wise

Sometimes an *ornamental name* was added to a first name. This was sometimes a fanciful creation of no particular meaning, and sometimes a nice sounding new surname was adapted from another name or combination of names. Sometimes circumstances caused an identifying surname to suddenly be needed. Some examples of ornamental surnames might be Blackburn, Greengood, or Monday. There are other origins for surnames, but most can be placed in some form under one of the categories you saw in Table 3.1, or classified as ornamental.

Are All the Smiths Related?

My grandmother firmly believed that all people who spelled their surname a certain way were related. Unfortunately for genealogists, this isn't usually the case. Sometimes you might find it to be true in the case of a very uncommon surname, but don't count on it even if you think your surname is unusual.

Smith is the most common surname in the United States (see the following figure), but there are probably hundreds of branches of Smiths that will never meet on any given Smith family tree. The reasons are many, but the short version is that the name's origin is probably a shortened version of a variety of occupations (black-smith, silversmith, goldsmith, wordsmith, and so on) from many different locations in the world. Add to that all the people who changed their names to Smith from another name for a variety of reasons (easier to pronounce than the original surname, evading the law, a slave taking the surname of a master, spelling or sur-name itself changed because of mistakes, and so on).

An online chart that shows the 50 most common U.S. surnames.

GRS-Library-Top 50 names in the United States - Microsoft Internet Explorer

File Edit View Favorites Tools Help

Top 50 names in the United States

United States Ranking	Surname	U. S. Ratio 1 to:	State Most Often Located in:	State Ratio 1 to:
1	Smith	157	Mississippi	68
2	Johnson	196	North Dakota	78
3	Williams	235	Mississippi	101
4	Brown	244	South Carolina	125
5	Jones	249	Mississippi	95
6	Miller	265	West Virginia	134
7	Davis	292	Mississippi	138
8	Wilson	372	Alabama	208
9	Anderson	378	North Dakota	126
10	Moore	407	Mississippi	187
11	Taylor	412	Mississippi	200
12	Martin	416	South Carolina	246

You can see why so many unrelated families can have the same surname or apparent variants or derivatives. A similar history can be applied to most other surnames, so don't assume that people with your surname are related to you or each other, even if they spell it exactly as you do.

Origins and Meanings

Sometimes the meaning of a name is obvious, especially if you're already certain of its geographic and ethnic origin. However, some names that may seem obvious may mean something entirely different, depending on where it actually came from. Other names may have no readily apparent meaning. You don't have to become an *onomastics* expert, but learning more about the origins and meanings of the surnames in your family can be interesting and a fun hobby in itself. Though it isn't usually necessary for genealogy, studying names may help provide clues to further research if at some point you find yourself at a standstill (the proverbial brick wall you'll see mentioned by other genealogists).

Learn to Misspell Names

On a What?

Onomastics is a scholarly term for the formal study of names of all kinds.

What's In a Name?

See *clanhuston.com/name/name.htm* for a brief history of surnames and a list of what hundreds of names actually mean.

You already learned that deliberately misspelling certain keywords can sometimes be useful when using search engines. This is especially true of surnames. Sometimes Web authors accidentally misspell names on their sites, and some surnames have a wide array of variant spellings due to a number of historical reasons. In the latter case, the names aren't actually misspelled, but if they're different from what you're accustomed to, they might as well be. Table 3.2 shows a list of some surnames and just a few ways they might be spelled. Use your imagination to come up with even more variations.

Table 3.2   Some Surnames and Variant Spellings

Surname	Variants
Stephens	Stevens, Stephans, Stephen, Stebbins
Smith	Smyth, Smythe, Smitt, Smiths
Perry	Parry, Perrin, Perrie
McClure	McLure, McClung, McClurg
Griggs	Grigg, Greggs, Grigsby

First Names and Nicknames

Surname Surfing

There are special Web sites to help you find your ancestors. If you'd like to practice, go to *surnameweb.org* and see if your surnames are listed.

If we lived in a perfect world, our ancestors would have easily classified *given names* (first names, sometimes called *Christian names* regardless of religion). They'd have names like Aaron, Bernard, and Charles; or Delilah, Elizabeth, and Felicia; and no two people with the same surname would have same first name. Additionally, each person would have an equally straightforward middle name and a nickname that actually described something about him or her. But that's only a dream, so let's wake up and learn the truth about our ancestors' names!

Is Verdell Male or Female?

Verdell was my paternal grandmother's first name, but I've also occasionally seen the same name (spelled the same way) used to refer to males in other family trees. So how do you tell the difference between certain male and female names? Ideally, you'll find and use primary records that include such information. But sometimes your first information might be clues you find online, and that information may not be complete.

Sometimes the key clue is a matter of how the name is spelled (as in *Francis* for males and *Frances* for females). Other names may be used for either gender or may be from an earlier era with which you're not familiar, so you need other clues if information you find doesn't specify the gender.

Non-Traditional Roles

In modern research you may encounter transgendered or multi-gendered individuals, or same-sex marriages. This opens a whole new can of worms for genealogists, regardless of personal views on any attendant religious, social, political, or moral issues. Such encounters will likely be extremely rare (if ever) during your research, but we'll discuss them briefly later in the book. Until then, we'll use the assumption that a person's gender is either male or female and that a marriage included one of each.

Was the Individual Married?

Perhaps the easiest clue to gender is the name of the person's spouse (assuming a marriage existed, that is). If the spouse's name is an obvious male name, the conclusion is that your person was female, and vice versa. If the person wasn't married or if their spouse's name isn't gender specific, you'll need other clues.

Did They Have a Middle Name?

What about the person's middle name? My grandmother Verdell would be no help there, because she didn't have a middle name. Though many weren't endowed with a middle name at all, most people born within the past two or three centuries were given middle names (sometimes more than one) at birth or christening. If your individual didn't have a middle name, you may need other clues. Sometimes an individual's initials can be misleading. For example, one person in my family tree had no given middle name, but at one point as a young man he made up an extra letter to fill out a document on which a middle initial was required. His new initials actually became his nickname, and he was called "N.T." for the rest of his life. But to the best of my knowledge, the *T* never represented any actual name or other meaning.

Other Clues to Gender

In modern times, it's common to find both men and women within almost any given occupation, but in older times, one gender or the other almost exclusively held certain jobs and careers. If you know a person's job or hobby, you may have a good clue to their gender. For example, if your individual was a carpenter or a blacksmith, the person was most likely male. If the person was a dressmaker or a spinner of yarn, you've more likely found a female.

If you still haven't determined an individual's gender, you may need to dig even deeper by seeking out resources to learn more about naming practices and traditions regionally and worldwide. Or perhaps the individual had a nickname that might give more clues. You'll learn more about these in the next section.

Nicknames May Surprise You

It may be widely known that *Charlie* is a common nickname for someone named Charles. But did you know that *Patsy* was once as common a nickname for the given name Martha as it was (and still is) for Patricia? One of my great-grandmothers was named Margaret, but she wasn't called *Madge* or *Maggie* or *Meg*. She didn't even have one of the more unusual sounding nicknames for Margaret such as *Daisy* or *Meta*; she was called *Lessie*. If I didn't already know the nickname was derived from her middle name (Celestia), I'd be really confused trying to figure that one out!

What Do Nicknames Mean to Us?

The reason we care so much about our ancestors' nicknames goes deeper than merely being interested in their personalities. Many times an individual's nickname (instead of the given name) was used for official documents and other records. Sometimes this was deliberate for whatever reason, and other times it may have been a mistake on the part of the person making the original record or a later transcript. In some cases, an ancestor's nickname is the only clue—name-wise, that is—we may have to their true identity.

Don't Assume Too Much

If you find nicknames like *Pat*, *Sam*, *Charlie*, or *Frankie*, don't assume these are all men or all women. *Pat* could be Patrick or Patricia; *Sam* might mean Samuel or Samantha; *Charlie* might be short for Charles or Charlotte; and *Frankie* might really be Franklin or Francine. These are but a few of the variations of just a few specific names and nicknames; there are lots more. Look at the list of nicknames on this Web page and you'll see what I mean: *www.uftree.com/UFT/HowTos/SettingOut/nickname1.html* (shown in the following figure).

Colorful Nicknames

Some nicknames (like "Pepper" or "Cotton") might give you clues to your ancestor's personality or a physical characteristic.

Nickname	Christian Name(s)
Bell, Bella, Belle	Arabelle, Anabelle, Isabel, Isabella, Rosabel
Bess, Bessie	Elizabeth
Beth	Elizabeth
Betsy, Betty	Elizabeth
Bitsy	Elizabeth
Bob, Bobby	Robert
Cindy	Cintha, Cynthia, Lucinda
Daisy	Margaret
Delia	Adelia, Adele, Cordelia
Dick	Richard
Dobbin	Robert
Dode, Dody	Dorothy, Theodore, Theodorick
Dora	Dorothy, Eudora, Theodora
Ed, Eddie, Eddy	Edgar, Edmund, Edward, Edwin, Edwina
Effie, Effy	Euphemia
Eliza	Elizabeth
Greta	Margaret, Margaretha
Ella, Ellie	Eleanor, Elenora
Fannie, Fanny	Frances

Loads of nickname lists like this might provide clues to given names.

Just because a name looks like a nickname, don't always assume it *is* a nickname—it may actually be a given name. My own name is a good example of this. Though *Terri* is a common nickname for Teresa, Terrell, and others, in my case it isn't a nickname at all; Terri is the name on my birth certificate. As a side note: I've been lucky enough to enjoy a good deal of humor due to people who ask, "What is Terri short for?" I smile and tell them that just because I'm short (in stature), it doesn't mean my name is!

Don't assume a nickname like *Junior* always means there's also a *Senior* somewhere, or vice versa. Sometimes these kinds of nicknames are used to differentiate a person with the same first name as someone else, but not necessarily within the same family. See the following Web sites for more information on first names, nicknames, surnames, and naming practices:

> www.hamrick.com/names
>
> www.tngenweb.usit.com/franklin/frannick.htm
>
> www.s-gabriel.org/docs/gennames.html
>
> www.s-gabriel.org/docs/modnames.html

Where Did Your Ancestors Live?

Now that you've decided *who* you're looking for, you need to know from *where* they came. In addition to finding out where they lived, you'll also want to know where they were born, where they died, and where they were buried. In some cases, you'll use locations as clues to find specific individuals when their name or other information isn't quite enough to pinpoint who they were.

Using Online Geographic Resources

Maps and *gazetteers* are not only useful, they're often considered indispensable to genealogists. If you happen to own a few nice fat and handsomely bound atlas-and-gazetteers full of large color maps, you're very fortunate. However, if you're like me and find that sort of expense beyond your budget, you'll be happy to know the Web is full of great geographic resources. Most cost little or nothing more than the time it takes to find and use them.

Come to Your Census

Maps can assist your research by helping you find census enumeration districts. (We'll discuss census records later in the book.)

Maps are most often used in genealogy as clues to where to find public or other records about an ancestor. For example, in the United States, county governments normally keep birth, death, property, and some other kinds of records. If you can identify the general region (or even better, the city, county, and state) where an ancestor lived, maps can help you find county seats, where relevant data about individuals may be obtained.

Some additional ways maps can help:

- Maps often reveal changed place names, especially when comparing older and newer maps of the same area. They may also show changes in the boundaries of states, counties, cities, and other subdivisions.

- Maps are useful for tracking the migratory patterns of individuals and family groups, and for finding ancestors who settled along one of the many well-known migration trails established in previous centuries.

- Maps may show locations or landmarks bearing names similar or even identical to certain surnames in your family. Sometimes this can lead to new or further discoveries in the area.

Hurry Up and Wait

Maps on the Web are comprised of image files, which usually take more time to load and sometimes use more system resources than average Web pages. This is especially true of interactive maps, some of which may use Java or similar applications to process your information requests. Be sure to have plenty of time and system resources free before using online maps!

Changed Boundaries and Place Names

As mentioned earlier, some geographic boundaries and place names may have undergone changes (or may no longer exist, in some cases) since your ancestors were there. Knowing specific instances can be helpful to resolve conflicting information on locations. For example, during a census, an ancestor may have been enumerated in a county or state whose boundary has since changed, or in a city or county that no longer exists.

If you were to use only one online geographic resource, it should probably be the *Geographic Names Information System* (GNIS), the United States' official database for place names. GNIS is a gazetteer maintained by the U.S. Geological Survey, and it often provides information on name changes, names of places that no longer exist, as well as other or secondary names for existing places. This system also contains the names of most types of geographic features. GNIS is especially useful for genealogical research because it even contains entries for small communities, churches, and cemeteries, some of which no longer physically exist.

GNIS isn't just a collection of maps, but there are map options on a large number of entries. You can find GNIS and other mapping and geographic resources on the Web site of the U.S. Geological Survey at *mapping.usgs.gov*.

Using the name of a place that no longer exists, I used GNIS to provide an example of one way it might be used. I imagined that I had limited data on an ancestor from a place called Benton somewhere in Alabama. For the example, we'll pretend I don't know if Benton is a town, county, or maybe a small unincorporated community, and suppose I don't yet know the place isn't there anymore. The following figure shows what the GNIS query form looks like when I've typed in what little information I know.

The GNIS query form and some completed input fields.

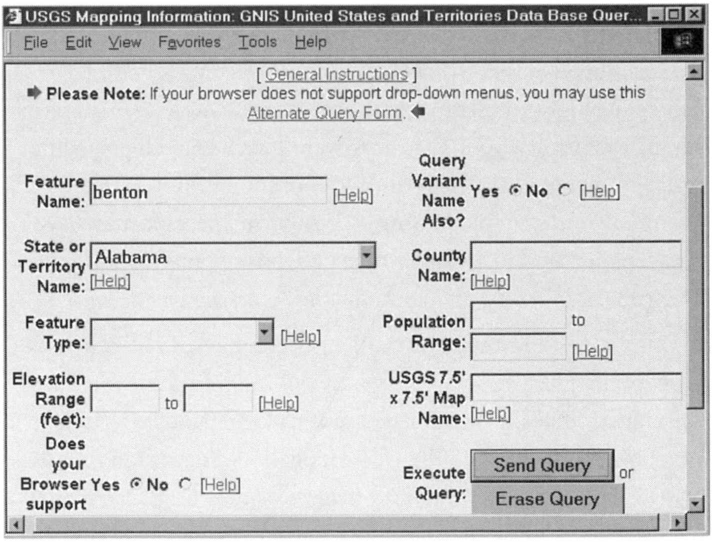

The next figure shows the results returned by GNIS after I click the Send Query button.

The GNIS query results based on my input.

Geographic Names Information System Query Results

BENTON, ALABAMA

10 Feature records have been selected from GNIS.*

Feature Name	St	County Name	Type	Latitude	Longitude	USGS 7.5' Map
Benton	AL	Lowndes	pop place	321824N	0864904W	Benton
Benton Landing	AL	Autauga	locale	321832N	0864840W	Benton
Benton Post Office	AL	Lowndes	post office	321820N	0864904W	Benton
Benton Round Mountain	AL	Marshall	summit	342736N	0863021W	Newsome Sinks
Benton-Collirene Division	AL	Lowndes	civil	321407N	0864604W	Collirene
Bentons Lake	AL	Bullock	reservoir	321013N	0854232W	Union Springs
Bentons Mill (historical)	AL	Cleburne	locale	335543N	0852910W	Borden Springs
Bentons Pond	AL	Barbour	reservoir	315208N	0851701W	Baker Hill
Calhoun County	AL	Calhoun	civil	334501N	0855100W	Jacksonville West
Elba	AL	Coffee	pop place	312452N	0860404W	Elba

As you see, there were a number of possibilities for me to explore. In the real world, I would explore each option until I found the information most relevant to me, but since I already knew the answer, I'll share it with you. The Benton I had in mind was once a county in Alabama, but it no longer exists by that name. Instead, surrounding county boundaries were moved to include the divided land into those counties as they exist today. The link marked *Calhoun County* would have given me the best information in this case. If you like, you can use my example to see the actual results online, or use your own query input to practice learning how to effectively use this valuable tool.

Landmark Hints

Suppose your ancestors lived near Sleeping Giant Mountain or beside Suck Creek (these really exist). You can find the locations with GNIS.

1. Connect to the Internet, open your Web browser, and enter *mapping.usgs.gov* into your browser's address or location bar.

2. Click the Geographic Names Information link. This takes you to a page with brief information about GNIS. Now click the Geographic Names Information System (GNIS) link found within the text.

3. Enter at least one search term (you can use my earlier example, if you like), then click the Submit Query button. You should then be shown a list of various results that you can explore at your leisure.

▼ **Try It Yourself**

▲

Migration Trails

As you progress in your research, you may find that some ancestors tended to settle in one place for a lifetime. You may be surprised to find that others appeared to move every few years.
Maybe a few even seemed to vanish into thin air, leaving few or
no clues as to what happened to them. Whether your ancestors
traveled a lot or only a little, you'll no doubt find that birds,
marine life, and plains animals aren't the only creatures that
migrate!

At Ancestry.com you'll find a huge selection of maps showing
major and minor migration trails as well as a wide variety of
other kinds of maps. Though many of the databases at
Ancestry.com are subscription based, these maps are free to
guests as well as members. To access them, type
www.ancestry.com/ancestry/maps.asp into your Web browser.

The following figure shows a portion of an 1863 map for
Chattanooga, Tennessee, and its surrounding area.

Maps can be use-
ful in tracking
your ancestors.

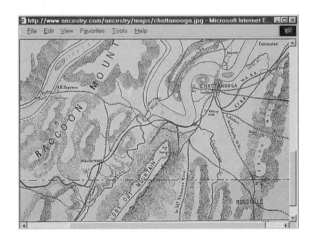

Try It Yourself ▼

1. Connect to the Internet, open your Web browser, and enter
   www.ancestry.com/ancestry/maps.asp into your browser's
   address or location bar.

2. Scroll down until you see the drop-down menu labeled State
   and County Maps. Click the down-arrow to the right, then
   highlight Chattanooga Region in Tennessee, Alabama, and
   Georgia, 1863. Now click the View button.

3. You'll be shown a small version of the map pictured in the preceding figure, but if you want to see the large version, just click directly on the small image.

If your ancestors migrated by rail, you'll probably want to see the Railroad Maps collection from the U.S. Library of Congress at *memory.loc.gov/ammem/gmdhtml/rrhtml/rrhome.html*. Even if you have no ancestral railroad travelers, many of these old maps are worth looking at for their beauty alone (see the next figure for an example).

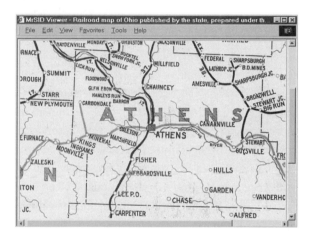

This Ohio railroad map is representative of others available, but they're prettier online.

Getting the Dates Right

Earlier in the book, we talked a bit about dates. No, you didn't miss the part about going out to dinners and movies with a charming companion—we're talking about the kind of dates that tell us *when* things happened. When you put time together with people and places, you're that much closer to the whole story!

Julian Versus Gregorian Calendars

The "Original" *Julian calendar* introduced by Julius Caesar dates from 44 B.C., when the length of the natural solar year was estimated to be 365 days and 6 hours. Every fourth year the extra six hours were collected and added as an extra day to the year, creating a leap year of 366 days. The calendar was revised about 325 A.D. (known as the "Old Style" Julian calendar), but it didn't fix

Going Local
The U.S. GenWeb Project (*www.usgenweb.org*) contains vast amounts of information among the hundreds of state and county Web sites within this huge network of volunteers.

the original error that caused the date of the Spring Equinox—a
naturally occurring regular event—to be earlier and earlier every
year. While this calendar was in use, March 25 was widely
accepted as the first day of the year.

In 1582, Pope Gregory XIII's astronomers determined that the
Julian calendar was off by 11 minutes and 14 seconds. The "New
Style" Julian calendar (now known as the *Gregorian calendar*)
came into existence. The astronomers reduced the number of leap
years so the average length of the calendar would be nearer to the
natural length of the solar year. The error was reduced from 11
minutes and 14 seconds a year to 26 seconds a year. Under this
system, January 1 was declared to be the first of the year.

But not all countries accepted this new calendar at the same time
(and some cultures and religious bodies still use other calendars).
England and the American colonies finally accepted the
Gregorian calendar in 1752. Before then, the government officially observed March 25 as the first of the year, but most people
celebrated January 1 as beginning of the new year. Thus, many
historians and other record-keepers (including genealogists)
include both years when writing dates that fall between January 1
and March 25 from 1752 and earlier. This method is called *double dating*. Table 3.3 shows some examples.

Table 3.3   Examples of Double Dating

Julian	Gregorian	Double Dating
31 Dec 1650	31 Dec 1650	31 Dec 1650/50
6 Jan 1699	6 Jan 1700	6 Jan 1699/00
14 Feb 1720	14 Feb 1721	14 Feb 1720/21
25 Mar 1730	25 Mar 1730	25 Mar 1730/30
1 Apr 1740	1 Apr 1740	1 Apr 1740/40

It's worth noting that not everyone uses the double dating method,
so be sure to pay special attention to recorded dates between
January 1 and March 25 prior to 1752. They may need to be
translated from a Julian date to Gregorian (or vice versa).

Other Dating Conventions

Other calendars include the Coptic calendar, Moslem calendar, Jewish calendar, Republican calendar, Indian calendar, and others. These aren't widely used for genealogical purposes, but you may find information pertinent to your individual research situation on the Chronology, Era and Calendars site at *www.bdl.fr/Granpub/ calendriers_eng.html*.

Wanna Practice?

If you haven't already practiced by looking at the Web sites mentioned in this chapter, go ahead and try them now. As you surf and/or practice searching, remember the tips you've learned and apply them to your practice sessions. Remember to bookmark sites to which you want to return later.

If you've already looked at the Web sites previously mentioned, you might enjoy further honing your research skills by practicing at one or more of these other sites:

> *geography.about.com* (About.com Geography)
>
> *www.rootsweb.com* (RootsWeb main page)
>
> *resources.rootsweb.com/surnames* (Surnames)
>
> *www.rootsweb.com/~canwgw* (Canada GenWeb)
>
> *worldgenweb.org* (World GenWeb)

The Bottom Line

You've learned the "WWW" basis for e-Genealogy: asking who, where, and when. In addition to some possible surprises you might have learned in this chapter, you should know

- The basics of surname history and how that can help give clues toward research.

- That the Web is rich with geographic resources to help with clues to find places where your ancestors were.

- That dates may not always be as obvious as they appear at first glance.

Workshop

Use the following workshop to help reinforce the knowledge you've gained in this lesson.

Q My grandmother says our Miller line was originally from England, but my father says they were from Germany. Who is right?

A Without knowing a great deal more detail, there's no way to know for sure. It may be that there are more than one line of Millers in your family, so both your grandmother and your father could be essentially correct. Then again, one or both might be wrong, depending on other factors.

Q I found that an ancestor had a child named Dorian. This was probably a boy, right?

A Not necessarily. Such a name might have been used for either gender, so without other information, it would be hard to know for sure. Until you do find out, it's a good idea to include a note saying what gender you think the child was and why you think so.

Q An old letter says that one of my ancestors was born in Madrid. Why can't I find him?

A Without knowing more clues, the place could be anywhere from the famous Madrid in Spain to any number of small towns or communities scattered across America, or the name may even refer to a hospital or other local landmark. It may be that the place name has since changed, or it may no longer exist at all. Try using one or more of the geographic resources online to help find your ancestor.

Quiz

Take the following quiz to see how much you've learned.

Questions

1. True or False: It's easier to find ancestors if the family has an uncommon surname.

2. Name at least three nicknames for Charles and at least three nicknames for Katherine.

3. True or False: A migration trail is what ancestors used when they wanted to watch birds fly north for the winter.

4. True or False: Most countries and cultures currently use the Julian calendar.

Answers

1. True. Though there will be exceptions, research is often less complicated when your surname is unusual.

2. *For Charles*: Buck, Carl, Chad, Charlie, Charley, Chaz, Chick, Chuck. *For Katherine*: Kathy, Karen, Katie, Kathleen, Kay, Kat, Kit, Kitsey, Kittie, Kitty, Trina. (Did you think of others not shown here?)

3. False. Your ancestors may indeed have been bird watchers, but for genealogical purposes we're only interested in migration trails left by humans.

4. False. Most currently use the Gregorian calendar.

CHAPTER 4

Has Someone Already Researched Your Family?

In earlier chapters you learned which tools you need for e-Genealogy, how to perform basic searches, and other basic knowledge and skills to form a solid foundation for your research. All this was intended to get you ready to dig deeper. You'll learn about finding and using vital records and other data online in the next few chapters. But before then, you'll probably want to be sure that you aren't going to "reinvent the wheel."

There's always the possibility that someone else has already researched all or part of your family history, and they may have published some or all of their findings online. This isn't to say that you should copy someone else's work to use as your own; that's considered a big no-no for obvious ethical—and often legal—reasons (we'll discuss these aspects of research in more detail later). However, you *can* use the work done by someone else as a starting point to refine and expand your own research.

This phase of your research may turn out to be the most fun and rewarding. You might be pleasantly surprised to find that a distant cousin or two have researched and published a good deal of your family tree, or you may find only tidbits of research on your ancestors. Then again, you may find no previous research at all on your family online. But you'll probably begin to network with other researchers and eventually find yourself trading information with one or more of them. At the very least, you'll be comforted by sharing frustrations with other researchers and you'll learn from the many others who share your interest in genealogy.

What You'll Learn in This Chapter:

▶ How to use personal genealogy Web sites effectively.

▶ How to use sites by non-profit and commercial organizations.

▶ When a bargain isn't always a bargain.

▶ How to find other researchers to talk to and exchange information with.

Learn to Search Web Sites

As you learned earlier, you'll find a list of great starting points in Appendix A, "Recommended Sites." However, don't rely *solely* on this list or on any other static site directory to find Web sites relevant to your research. Apply the techniques you've learned about search engines and online site directories to broaden your possibilities. These are able to update their indexes more often than any printed list could ever hope to do.

You'll see the term *GEDCOM* repeatedly as you travel the Web, so it's a good idea to become familiar with it now. GEDCOM is an acronym for *GE*nealogical *D*ata *COM*munications, a standard format for special text files to be imported and/or exported by most current genealogy software. This makes it easy for researchers to share data. You can even read a GEDCOM in its raw form with any word processor. If you'd like to read the technical stuff about GEDCOMs, see *www.tiac.net/users/pmcbride/ gedcom/55gctoc.htm.*

Searching Personal Sites

Little Engines

Some Web sites have their own internal search engines, which can often make such sites easier to use.

Searching personal genealogy sites can sometimes be frustrating. There is no standard regarding what and how much information is published or how it is presented. Some sites are as simple as one plain text page showing only a short list of the family's major surnames. Others contain hundreds of bright, flashy pages with unknown amounts of information and data, photographs, link lists, more animated graphics than you can shake a stick at, and music that may make you want to mute your speakers. Some sites have too few site navigation links or buttons, and others have so many that they seem to outnumber actual content.

Luckily, most personal sites fall somewhere between the extremes I mentioned (see the following figure for a good example). You'll want to develop a regular routine to help you search these sites effectively. In addition to helping you glean information and data, a regular search routine will help you to establish and maintain good documentation habits.

Simplicity by design is often the key to elegance and usefulness.

Your individual research routine may vary slightly in actions or the order in which you perform them, but you might pick up some ideas based on my own methods;

- If I find a site by using a search engine, I first quickly glance through the page. I do this to check that the content didn't change to an entirely different topic after being indexed in the search engine; this can and does happen sometimes.

- If the quick glance-through looks promising, I read more thoroughly or use my browser's Find function to search the page for the same keyword(s) I originally used with the search engine.

- If I find my keyword(s) or anything else that looks potentially relevant to my research, I check to see if the author offers a GEDCOM file or Web version database, any pedigree lists or charts, or similar data.

- If I find relevant information of any kind, I make notes of what it is and where I found it, then I look for the author's email address. If I find no information, I make a note of that, too. This means I won't accidentally look at that same site a week or two later (though I do later revisit sites that I feel *may* eventually include more information).

Don't Forget "Find"

Use your browser's Find function (Edit, Find) when it makes sense to do so (for example, to search for specific keywords on a very large page).

- When I've recorded the author's email address I return to the information I found and record in detail whatever is there.

- Next I email the author to thank him or her; at the same time, I might also ask if they have other information not published online and/or offer data I have in which they may be interested. If there are inconsistencies between their data and what I already have, I let him or her know. Most genealogists are happy to work with others to ensure correct data for all parties involved.

- Depending on the type and amount of information I find, my next step is to verify its accuracy by looking up primary and/or secondary records; sometimes I wait until I obtain more details on an individual. I repeat this process with each personal site I visit, with occasional variations depending on the actual content at any given site.

Sites by Non-Profit Organizations

Cyndi Sorts It Out for You

Among the many other resources for finding personal genealogy sites, you might find Cyndi's List helpful (*www.cyndislist.com/personal.htm*).

Sometimes your best bet for information might be through sites run by non-profit or not-for-profit groups and organizations. These include genealogical and historical societies, volunteer groups, family associations, and of course, the ever popular and helpful Family History Department of the Church of Jesus Christ of Latter-Day Saints (LDS). Some organizations charge nominal fees or membership dues for research help or materials, and others offer help or information totally free of charge.

Genealogical and Historical Societies

More and more Web sites by local and regional genealogical and historical societies are appearing online. These can often be especially helpful when you have a large number of ancestors from a given area. These societies vary as to what types of services they offer, how much information is available on their sites, and what kinds of fees or membership dues they require (if any). But most offer research assistance in some form. You'll need to check the sites of the societies in which you're interested to see what specific services they offer.

One good resource to locate these kinds of sites is from Illya D'Addezio's Society Hill directory at *www.daddezio.com/society* (shown in the following figure). You might also find your local society's Web site listed in phone books, newspapers, or other local publications. If you can't find the genealogical or historical society you're looking for by using typical search methods, try searching local or regional online library catalogs or community search features. (I've found university library sites especially useful for this.) You can often find contact information for smaller local societies that aren't listed in phone books and that don't have Web sites of their own.

Directory of genealogy and history societies in the U.S., Canada, and Australia.

Volunteer Groups

Thank goodness for fellow researchers who are willing to offer information and help to others! Genealogists are among the most friendly and generous of folks, and the growing number of volunteer genealogy help sites is good evidence of that.

Some volunteer-based sites present a wealth of information and data online at no charge, as does the GenWeb network of sites I've mentioned before. In some ways these are similar to genealogical and historical societies, but they are much less formal organizations. These sites typically offer (in varying degrees) surname resources based on specific regions, local history

Small Bytes

Don't abuse the generosity of others by asking too much at one time. Request assistance in small amounts.

resources for the area, and a variety of records and documents such as census data, military records, wills, deeds, family bibles, and so on.

Other sites are based on volunteers that offer individual research help in varying degrees, usually for free or nominal charges to cover the volunteer's expense. Perhaps the largest network of this type of site is The Genealogy Helplist at *posom.com/hl*. Another great resource is Genealogy's Most Wanted at *www.citynet.net/mostwanted* (shown in the following figure). There are many others similar to these, so use your search skills to find them. Whatever sites you find and choose to use, be sure to read and follow any special instructions they have in order to make your experience as productive as possible.

Find your "most wanted" or ask for research help at GMW.

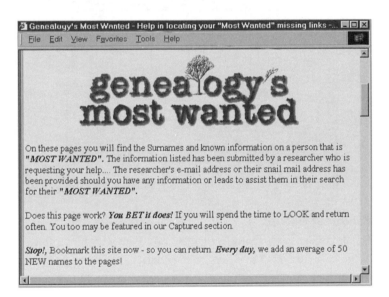

Family Associations

Family associations are usually based on a single surname, and most are involved in genealogical pursuits in addition to other family matters. Some groups are local or regional, and others may cover all areas in which a particular family line ever existed. Still others specialize in *one-name studies*; they compile information and data on all known variants of one surname, regardless of location or whether all the individuals within the families are actually related. Many family associations have quite helpful Web sites online, and more are being published as time goes by.

Similar to genealogical societies, what you can obtain from family associations will vary, and membership dues are often required. Perhaps the easiest way to find an existing association and/or Web site is to ask family members. If they don't know, you can see if your surname is listed at *www.angelfire.com/ks/ windshipgenhelp/family.html* or *www.one-name.org*. If your family name isn't listed on these, you can try using search engines or other Web directories.

FamilySearch.org

The long-awaited site for the famous LDS Family History Centers found in various locations around the world finally arrived on the Web in mid-1999. Though the amount of information and data available from the site is nowhere near as extensive as what you'll find at the physical FHC locations, there's a lot there! The most popular search option uses data from the Ancestral File™, International Genealogical Index® (IGI), and thousands of Web sites. Like the physical FHCs, you don't have to be a member of the LDS Church and there is no charge to access the information. You can find FamilySearch at *familysearch.org*.

As an example of how you might use FamilySearch, imagine that I had an ancestor named Abraham Lincoln who was married to a lady named Mary Todd (it's okay to laugh if you want to). The following figure shows what the main screen looks like when I've typed the names in the appropriate entry fields.

The IGI Is...

The world's largest collection of genealogical records. They were submitted by individual researchers or extracted from original records.

When I clicked the Search button, I was shown a list of results. There were six results from the IGI, one from the Ancestral File, and several Web sites I could look at. I chose the link from the Ancestral File result and was shown the basic data on the individual (Mr. Lincoln). On that page I was also given the option to look at pedigree charts or family group records for the individuals shown on the page. The next figure shows the top portion of the family group record for ol' Honest Abe himself (there's much more when you scroll down the page online). I never realized he had so many children!

The main FamilySearch screen with my keywords entered.

The FamilySearch family group record for Abraham Lincoln.

Normally you'll see family group records within the FamilySearch frame, but for a simplified illustration I took the screenshot with this group record page outside the frame. Other search options include using keywords (instead of names) or using a Custom Search to limit your results to either the Ancestral File, the IGI, or Web sites. You can also choose to browse the categories if you're not quite sure what you're looking for.

1. Suppose you find that one of your ancestors was named Mary Beckwith, whose father was Warren Beckwith. Go to *familysearch.org*, enter their names into the appropriate search fields, and click the Search button.

2. You should be shown several results. Click the link from the Ancestral File, which takes you to Mary's Individual Record. From there, you can see more information for her, including who her mother was. Now click on the Family button to the right of Mary's name.

3. Now you're shown a Family Group Record for Mary's parents and the rest of her immediate family. Are you beginning to suspect that one of Mary's ancestors was a famous U.S. president? See if you can find your way through more of Mary's line to find out.

▼ **Try It Yourself**

Online Subscription-Based Services

Subscription-based services often provide a good deal of free and useful information, but you'll ultimately have to pay for more detailed or specialized data. The best of these sites offer free trials or demos; I would personally be wary of any service (of any kind) that required payment up front before I had any real idea what I was paying for. From what I've experienced, the fees for these aren't as expensive as you might think (actual costs vary according to specific services and subscription options). You'll find other subscription-based services by using search techniques, but following are two popular ones:

Family Practice

You can practice using FamilySearch and other sites by looking for previous research on members of a famous family.

- Ancestry.com (*ancestry.com*) offers a wide array of free information and data. Free services include your own customized email address, articles and newsletters, Web site directory, and access to certain databases. Subscribing members also receive access to all other databases, including census records; birth, marriage and death records; land and other property records; military records; obituaries and death indexes; genealogical books and publications, and more. In addition, members receive special purchase offers from Ancestry.com's online store.

- GenServ (*www.genserv.com*) specializes in one thing: GEDCOM files (and they have thousands of them, including some that aren't available elsewhere). Members request information and receive reports that tell which GEDCOMs their names appear in, if any. If there's a match, the appropriate GEDCOM file(s) may then be obtained. This service is quite inexpensive, but in addition to the subscription fee, you must submit your own GEDCOM file to add to their database in order to participate.

Family History Publications Online

Sometimes you might be lucky enough to find an old family history book that has been lovingly transcribed and published on someone's Web site (hopefully a public domain book, meaning no copyright laws were violated). The Web isn't exactly teeming with these because of the time and other resources involved, but a few are out there. You're much more likely to find bibliographies and similar lists of genealogy-related books and other publications (some rare or otherwise hard-to-find), some of which you might be able to purchase online. Here's another chance to practice and refine your Internet search skills.

Book 'Em, Danno!
For ideas (or specific titles) for books about your surname or region, check out Books We Own at *www.rootsweb.com/ ~bwo.*

In addition to information on books, you can find several genealogical magazines and hundreds (maybe thousands) of genealogy articles online. Many newspapers have local genealogy columns, and a good number of these are also represented on the Web sites of their respective newspapers. These publications are usually quite easy to find by using search engines. For example, try using the keyword phrase *genealogy magazines* in a couple of search engines to see what you come up with.

When Is a Bargain Not a Bargain?

You're in a grocery store and you see a sign that reads, "Asparagus 2 bunches for a dollar, regular $3 each! Get them while supplies last!" Excited, you grab two bunches (hey, you don't want the supply to run out before you get your share). You pay for your bounty, all the while feeling great about finding such a bargain. When you arrive home, reality sets in. You realize the asparagus isn't as fresh as the picture on the sign represented, plus no one in your household even likes asparagus! So did you truly get a bargain?

Off-the-Rack Genealogies

Companies that claim to have "pre-researched" family history books, coats of arms, or similar products to sell you should be looked at with the same care that you would use when determining a true bargain at a grocery store. Most of these products are not all they claim to be; more often they contain generic text and artistic representations with your surname inserted where appropriate. Direct mail is the usual method of advertising these "once in a lifetime" offers (some also advertise online), so you don't even get to see or handle a real sample of the product. Typically, whatever information these kinds of products contain can be easily found on your own at no charge.

So even if the cost is relatively low, it's up to you to determine whether any of these products are actually bargains. If you buy, be sure they have a reasonable return policy in case you're not satisfied.

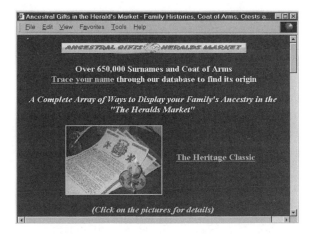

Products about ancestry are often pretty, but not always accurate.

If It Sounds Too Good to Be True...

You've no doubt heard the saying, "If it sounds too good to be true, it probably is." You should be wary of any company or individual who offers to find information for you as long as you pay a hefty fee in advance, especially if they use terms like "fool-proof" or "guaranteed." Before agreeing to anything, be sure to ask questions, search the Web to find more information, and seek out the experiences of previous clients whenever possible.

The Internet's Greatest Asset: Other People

Just as genealogy itself is more than mere facts and dry data, so are the resources you'll find online. The facts we find and use represent real people with real lives, and e-Genealogy would be much harder (if not impossible) and less interesting without real people to give it life and enhance it with color.

Good Feelings

It's tremendously satisfying to offer a casual suggestion to someone and have them respond, "Thanks! I never thought of that!"

You might find distant cousins or research companions by using personal genealogy sites, but you might also enjoy interacting with a larger number of fellow family history enthusiasts by using a more direct approach. How can you network with genealogists in large numbers without attending big genealogy conferences? Why, on the Internet, of course!

Email Discussion Groups

The number of available genealogy email discussion groups (sometimes called *listservs*) is already staggering, and more are being added all the time. You'll find lists that specialize in specific surnames, genealogy software, geographic regions, military history, local history, ethnic research, and other specialized or more general topics. Each specific list has its own rules and instructions to subscribe, so be sure to read up on these at the host site. What they all have in common is that people ask questions, seek opinions, request specific information, and share answers, opinions, and information with each other.

If you've never subscribed to an email list before, there are a few things you should be aware of. Some lists will only have small amounts of sporadic traffic while others will generate enough email to fill your mailbox daily. Subscribing to several different lists will increase the volume of email you receive, so be sure you don't bite off more than you can chew. I suggest beginning with one general topic email list first, then subscribe to a few other lists for specific surnames or other topics when you get used to how email lists work. Before posting to your lists, be sure you've read and understand their guidelines and rules, and even then just read the list email for a while until you become familiar with accepted forms of communication.

Of the many other email discussion groups available, the largest and oldest host for genealogy lists is RootsWeb. They have literally thousands of different lists to choose from. Among these is the oldest existing genealogy email list, ROOTS-L. To browse the list categories, go to *www.rootsweb.com/~maillist*.

Can the Spam

It's not nice (and in some cases, it's illegal) to send unsolicited email *of any kind* to large numbers of people at one time.

To use genealogy discussion groups effectively, be sure you:

- Read and follow instructions and rules for each list.

- Use brief but descriptive subject lines (not generic lines like "genealogy" or "my surnames" or "I have a question").

- Include your email address in your messages. Automatic signatures are usually accepted, but a tagline over four lines long is greatly frowned upon.

- Include all pertinent information when requesting specific information, but don't include unnecessary details (keep your messages brief when possible).

- Include a quote of relevant parts of a post to which you're replying. This helps to keep the topic in context. *Don't* include the entire post as a quote unless the post is very brief.

- Think twice before including your home address or phone number in a message. If you want to exchange this sort of personal information with other researchers, it's better to do so by private email between those parties only.

- Refrain from asking for information you can find on your own with a little effort (some people become resentful of what they consider wasteful posts). For example, instead of asking what county a town is in, you can usually find out easily by looking it up with an online geographic resource.

- When people reply to your posts, do thank them, but don't inundate the list with a separate thank-you note for each person who replied. If you like, send each person a separate private email instead.

Message Boards

Message boards are very similar to email discussion groups, but instead of coming to your mailbox, the messages are posted on the Web. Some boards also offer the option to send messages to your mailbox. Like email lists, message boards are available for general genealogy topics as well as a wide variety of specialized and more specific topics. Message boards may also be called *forums*, *bulletin boards*, or *query boards*. If you've never used a message board before, follow the same advice for email discussion groups to use these forums effectively.

You'll find genealogy message boards scattered all over the Web, sometimes as part of a personal site or as parts of volunteer and commercial sites. As with email groups, these forums will vary in how active they are. One site you might like to try is GenForum, which features hundreds of genealogy forums based on specific surnames, specific geographic locations, and other topics. You can find these at *genforum.familytreemaker.com* (an example is shown in the following figure).

Stephens researchers can interact here (there's also a Stevens forum).

Chat Rooms

Chat rooms are somewhat similar to email discussion groups and message boards in that you interact with real people. The exception is that this interaction is in real time (that is, it's live). If you're a veteran of other kinds of chat, you'll have no trouble with genealogy chat rooms. However, if you've never chatted before, you might find yourself overwhelmed at how fast it can sometimes go, especially if your typing speed isn't fairly fast. But hang in there! You'll get used to it with practice, and I found that chatting actually helped to increase my typing speed.

Organized chats can be useful for trading data or other information, but informal chats are better for the social aspects of getting to know other genealogists, laughing at jokes, and letting off steam when you're frustrated by your research. Long-lasting friendships are often formed in chat rooms, and you may even find cousins you never knew existed!

Engine Failure?
Don't use search engines to find chat rooms. You'll find too many pornographic and other irrelevant sites among the search results. Web directories are much more helpful in this case.

Know Your Netiquette

Netiquette is just what it sounds like: etiquette for the Net. It's important to know at least the basic rules of netiquette to help your online interactions go as smoothly as possible. Since people who communicate electronically (via email, message boards, or chat rooms) can't see each other's faces or body language, sometimes it's hard to tell in what spirit or context they may mean something they say. This can sometimes lead to misunderstandings, which can in turn lead to arguments that result in hurt feelings. Generally accepted conventions have been developed to help avoid such situations.

The first rule of netiquette is to think about what you want to say, write it as concisely as possible, then read what you've written before you send it or post it. In some cases you might need to read it a second time and think about it again before sending it to cyberland. If you're making a humorous comment, try to let your tone of writing show it. Also use *emoticons* to help convey your tone, if necessary. Emoticons are "icons" that represent emotions, usually represented by common keyboard symbols. One of the most often used is a simple *smiley*, represented by :-) (a colon, a dash, and a parenthesis). You can find lists of an amazing variety of other emoticons all over the Web. The following figure shows an example.

More smileys and frownies than you're ever likely to need.

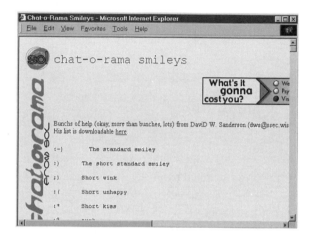

Don't Get Burned

Online interactions can sometimes turn into "flames" (mis-understandings can result in a war of words). Don't add fuel to the fire by participating.

Avoid typing your messages in ALL CAPS whenever possible. This is considered "shouting" by most online veterans, which means it's generally considered rude behavior. It also makes even important messages hard to read for most people. The exception is *do* use caps for SURNAMES or when you want to EMPHA-SIZE a word or phrase.

Most email discussion groups, message boards, and some chat rooms have a rule about staying on topic. Some are stricter than others and enforce the rule to differing degrees. Whatever the specifics are for the interactions in which you choose to partici-pate, be sure to stay on topic, even if others don't. For example, unless you're designated to do so, it won't help to publicly point out that someone else is breaking the off-topic rule; you'll only be adding to the broken rule with an off-topic post of your own.

When someone helps you, thank him or her. Don't go overboard, but don't neglect to acknowledge the generosity of others. At the same time, if you help someone else, don't take it personally if they neglect to thank you. Some people are slower than others to do this, or there may be unavoidable circumstances that prevent them from doing so.

The most important rule? Relax, have fun, and enjoy yourself as you make new friends, meet new relatives, and find your family online!

The Bottom Line

You've learned get a head start by determining whether someone has already researched your family. In addition to some possible surprises you might have learned in this chapter, you should know

- How to get a head start by searching various kinds of genealogy Web sites.

- To be cautious of questionable genealogical bargains to avoid possibly getting (or at least feeling) ripped off.

- How interactive functions allow you to network and trade information with other researchers. And you'll have fun at the same time!

Workshop

Use the following workshop to help reinforce the knowledge you've gained in this lesson.

Q I found a great-looking Web site, but the pages are so large! How can I find information there without reading for days?

A Sometimes reading is the only way to know for sure what's there. However, you can usually speed up your search by using your Web browser's Find function, using various keywords and spellings just as you would with a search engine.

Q A company called Halbert's claims to have a book about my surname. Is this a good deal?

A My personal opinion is that these books aren't worth the price, but the choice is ultimately up to you. I suggest searching the Web for information on the company and other people's experiences with them before deciding.

Q I went to a chat room where everyone was talking, but no one talked to me. Why?

A Did you ask questions or introduce yourself? It may be that the other participants were respecting your privacy and felt you would enter the conversation when you felt comfortable. After all, conversation is a two-way street (or in the case of some chat rooms, a multi-lane highway)!

Quiz

Take the following quiz to see how much you've learned.

Questions

1. True or False: Personal genealogy sites don't usually have much really useful information.

2. Name at least three online resources where you might find research already done on your family.

3. True or False: Email discussion groups are similar to message boards.

4. True or False: If you want to say something important, you should type in ALL CAPS.

Answers

1. False. Though they vary in scope, sometimes these can be your most productive resources for information on specific people and families.

2. Personal Web sites, sites by genealogical and historical societies, sites by volunteer groups, family association sites, FamilySearch.org, online subscription-based services,

genealogy publications and articles, genealogy email discussion groups, genealogy message boards, and genealogy chat rooms. (Did you think of others not named here?)

3. True. Though the posting and reading methods differ, the guidelines for using them are very similar.

4. False. Capitalized surnames and emphasized words and phrases are okay, but typing in ALL CAPS for everything in a message is considered bad netiquette.

PART III

Databases and Records Collections Online

CHAPTER 5

Exploring Government Records Online

If only life was like the movies. As the hero of your story, you need information on some people who keep evading you. No problem. Just tap into the handy dandy computer system maintained by the government for that purpose—if you know how, that is, and heroes always do. Next thing you know, you're saying, "Aha! I have you now!"

Despite the prevalence of that kind of scenario in films and other fiction, that isn't the way it works. You'll find some kinds of records in great abundance on the Net, and some will remain harder to find. Still other records aren't online at all, and might never be.

You can sometimes find electronically reproduced (scanned) copies of official documents and records on the Internet, but more often you'll find transcriptions of original data. You'll find a variety of formats for these transcripts; some will contain data copied directly from the originals and others will be abstracts or samples from originals presented according to the whims of the transcribers. Some records are well organized in good-sized collections, and others are scattered here and there like proverbial needles in Internet haystacks.

Although you can't just tap a few keys and log in to secret government computer systems, you'll have something in common with the movie hero who can. You'll likely have to work harder than he does, but when you do find data online about your ancestors, you'll probably feel like saying, "Aha! I have you now!" Getting results is what a hero does, after all. And you don't even have to sweat.

What You'll Learn in This Chapter:

▸ What vital records are and how important they are to your research.

▸ How census records can help find ancestors.

▸ Some other legal records you might find online.

Vital Records

Vital records reflect the most vital events in a person's life. Every person is born and every person eventually dies. Add to that the fact that most people marry at least once, and you have the basis of vital records: birth, marriage, and death records. Vital records are important to family historians for several reasons. Because these are official government documents, care has been taken to maintain them with as high a degree of accuracy as possible. Errors can and do exist, but vital records are sometimes the only source of information about certain ancestors.

Vital records weren't required to be kept in the United States until early in the 20th century, but some do exist earlier than that. These records are required by the U.S. federal government, but they're not kept at that level. States and counties are responsible for recording and maintaining birth, marriage, and death certificates. You might need other sources for information pertaining to births, marriages, and deaths prior to the late 19th century, if official government documents can't be found (we'll discuss "unofficial" records later).

The term primary record is sometimes used interchangeably with the term vital record, but this isn't entirely accurate. Whereas vital records are considered primary, not all primary records are considered vital.

A *primary record* is one that documents an event on or very near the occurrence of the event itself (for example, a death certificate recorded on the occasion of a death or a deed recorded during a land transaction). A *secondary record* is one that documents an event by "hearsay." For example, an ancestor's will might mention his children's names and ages, which can give clues to their birth dates. However, the information probably won't be as accurate or as complete as an official birth record for each child mentioned.

Sometimes secondary records might be all you can find for a given individual. In that case, try to verify any data you find with any other information sources you can find that contain similar data. If primary vital records do exist for the individual, obtain copies to add to your research collection rather than relying on secondary material.

Death Records

Death records are sometimes the best place to begin searching for further information on an ancestor. If you know a person's full name, date of death, and place of death, you can usually obtain a death certificate for that person.

Some death certificates contain more details than others do, but you're likely to find a good deal more than just death-related information. You'll probably learn the person's age at death (sometimes the birth date), birthplace, marital status (sometimes the spouse's name), occupation, and parents' names (sometimes the mother's maiden name). Some death certificates may contain even more, such as citizenship information, cause of death, attending physician, and so on. A death certificate is a primary record for the event of a death, but for other information it is secondary in nature.

Birth Records

Most modern birth certificates show the person's name, date and place of birth; parents' names, ages, and birthplaces; parents' residence and occupation(s); attending physician; and often the number of other children born to the mother. Some might contain even more information.

Birth records are considered by most scholars to be the most reliable of the primary record sources because the information is usually given by those who know it best (the mothers and fathers themselves). However, be aware that errors can and do occur, or data may be inaccurate for other reasons. For example, false names might have been used in some cases of illegitimate birth. Sometimes births were recorded during religious rituals such as christening or baptism rather than on or near the actual birth date; in these cases, there may sometimes be inaccuracies due to the passage of time between the event and the record.

Vital Help

In addition to using search techniques we've already talked about, you might find the following site helpful for finding vital records: *vitalrec.com*.

Getting Religious

For ancestors born before the 20th century, church or other religious records might be your best bet for birth info.

Marriage and Divorce Records

Every state in the U.S. required some form of marriage registration when counties within each state were formed (except New York, Pennsylvania, and South Carolina, where marriage records weren't required until the 1880s). The type of records created and exactly what and how much information they contain vary from place to place. At the least, marriage certificates will likely tell you the names of the bride and groom, the date and place of the marriage, and who performed the ceremony. Some records also include the ages of the bride and the groom, the birthplace of each, occupation(s), parents' names, residence, and witnesses to the marriage.

These days, a high percentage of marriages end in divorce, but divorce itself isn't a modern invention. Divorce records can be valuable genealogical documents. Modern divorce certificates can be obtained from some state vital record offices, but the case files (which contain more detailed information) will be found in whatever local court heard the divorce suit. Ask the county clerk where the divorce was filed to which court you should direct your request. Most case files include the names of the divorcing couple, date and place of marriage, ages and/or birth dates and places, minor children and their ages, and the grounds for divorce. The record may also include names of other family members.

Census Records

Federal census records have been maintained in the United States since 1790, and they can provide countless clues to genealogists seeking extra (or sometimes *any*) information on their ancestors. The records from the 1890 census were largely destroyed (partly by fire and partly by later bureaucratic blunders), but salvaged records containing over 6,000 names were placed on microfilm, so don't automatically dismiss that census year as a waste of your time. After all, those folks are *someone's* ancestors.

Computer Genealogy?

The Eleventh Census (1890) was the first U.S. census to use Herman Hollerith's electrical tabulation system. That is, it was the first census in which a computer was used. That computer, as simple as it was, greatly sped up the task, and it was a direct ancestor of the PC sitting on your desk!

What You Can Learn from Them

Federal population censuses in the United States have been taken *decennially* (every 10 years) since 1790. Information found in these records could lead to other sources necessary for complete research, such as court, immigration, land, military, naturalization, and vital records. The first six censuses contain less data than later ones, but they still contain helpful clues that can be used. For a quick reference of what you can find on records from each census year, bookmark this page from the USGenWeb Census Project:

www.rootsweb.com/~usgwcens/help/questions.html (shown in the following figure).

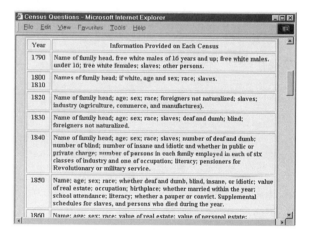

A handy guide to what you'll find in which census years.

Early census records provided the names of only the heads of households, and no exact ages were mentioned (age ranges were used instead). This is somewhat sparse information, but it can at least give general clues useful for tracking the head of household from one census to the next and for estimating the composition of the family (which should be confirmed by other records).

Beyond the Feds

Many states conducted their own censuses during different years, plus there are several existing census records dating from Colonial times.

Later records include names and ages of all members of the household, plus the birthplace of each. Some records may contain clues to search immigration records and for possible naturalization records. Later census records also usually include occupations, which can lead to further sources of data. For example, if household members were farmers, you'll know to check for deeds, mortgages, and property tax records. It's a good idea to check all existing records for any place ancestors are known to have lived. If nothing else, census records will tell you where they lived during given enumeration periods. For even more census information, see NARA's Genealogy Page at *www.nara.gov/genealogy*.

A small portion of the 1850 Federal Census for Autauga County, Alabama.

How to Find Them

You'll find fragments of census data scattered among thousands of personal genealogy Web sites, but there are also some centralized locations to find records online. In addition to the USGenWeb Census Project mentioned earlier, you might also include *www.census-online.com/links* in your bookmarks. Both sites contain many of the same links to data, but there may be times when one has more than the other. Of course, don't forget that there may also be other good transcripts of census records that those haven't listed yet, so sharpen those Web search skills!

Other Records

In addition to census and vital records, there are many other "official" records to help give you clues about the details of your ancestors' lives and deaths. Some of these aren't precisely government records, but the ones we'll discuss here are all legal documents of one kind or another.

Census Specials

There were several periodic special census schedules to enumerate agricultural, manufacturing, slave, Indian (Native American), freedmen, and other groups.

The Social Security Death Index

The Social Security Death Index (SSDI) can be a handy way to look up preliminary information on people who have died within about the past 50 years. Armed with what you learn from the SSDI, you'll be better prepared with clues to search for appropriate vital and other records for an ancestor.

The SSDI is generated from the U.S. Social Security Administration's (SSA) Death Master File. It contains records of deceased persons who had Social Security numbers *and* whose deaths were reported to the SSA. In most cases a report of death was made in connection with Social Security death benefits, but if a family didn't claim benefits or didn't report the death of an individual for whatever reason, that individual probably won't show up in the index. People who didn't have a Social Security Number at the time of death are never included in the SSDI.

The information you can usually expect to learn from the SSDI is the person's name, birth date, death date, last residence, last benefit location, Social Security Number, and where and when the number was issued.

Searching this index is similar to performing Web searches; if you don't find your person the first time, try different spellings or change other search criteria until you've exhausted the possibilities. For example, I searched for one of my grandfathers, knowing that he had a Social Security Number and that benefits were claimed. However, I had a bit of trouble finding him listed. After trying different searches, I finally found him. He was listed by first initial (instead of his full first name) and the database showed an incorrect state for his last residence, so I was thrown off track for a while.

For even more information on the SSDI and tips for using it, see *www.ancestry.com/research/ssdi.htm* (you can also perform free searches of their version of the SSDI while you're at the Ancestry.com site). The following figure shows the search input screen for this SSDI. I used my father-in-law's name and the state of his last known residence for this example.

Ancestry.com's SSDI search screen with my example entered.

An SS-5 Is...

An original application for Social Security benefits. It might reveal a good deal of information for your ancestor.

The next figure shows the first results screen from my search (I made sure to use the bottom *Search* button on the first screen so that any advanced search input would be included). I got 16 results, but depending on your search criteria, you may get fewer or more results for an individual.

The correct person in this case is the one listed next to last. You can click on the Write Letter link to generate a request for the individual's original application (SS-5), which contains much more detailed information. The SSA charges a fee for this ($7.00 when the SSN is known or $16.50 for a full records search if you don't know the number).

SSDI search results based on my example.

Name	Birth	Death	Last Residence	Last Benefit	SSN	Issued	
JAMES LAMB	19 Jan 1909	Sep 1974	37091 Chapel Hill, Marshall, TN		411-16-2507	TN (Before 1951)	Write Letter
JAMES LAMB	19 Apr 1894	Sep 1976	37160 Shelbyville, Bedford, TN		414-16-1893	TN (Before 1951)	Write Letter
JAMES LAMB	16 Oct 1913	Jan 1978	37130 Murfreesboro, Rutherford, TN		410-01-0340	TN (Before 1951)	Write Letter
JAMES LAMB	28 Jan 1935	Jun 1979		37130 Murfreesboro, Rutherford, TN	411-56-5931	TN (1953)	Write Letter
JAMES LAMB	21 Sep 1923	Mar 1984	37303 Athens, Mc Minn, TN	37303 Athens, Mc Minn, TN	402-28-4548	KY (Before 1951)	Write Letter
JAMES LAMB	16 Jun 1914	Feb 1986	37405 Chattanooga, Hamilton, TN	37405 Chattanooga, Hamilton, TN	413-01-5733	TN (Before 1951)	Write Letter
JAMES LAMB	30 Apr 1933	17 May 1988	37160 Shelbyville, Bedford, TN		413-48-0161	TN (Before 1951)	Write Letter

State and Territory Death Indexes

State and territory death indexes are similar to the SSDI, but the information to be gained from them will vary somewhat from one location to another (some provide more data than others do). I'm not currently aware of a free public database that covers all such indexes, but you can find partial transcriptions on various genealogy sites run by volunteer groups or individuals, and some of the subscription-based services offer larger collections of death index databases. Here's yet another chance to sharpen those Web search skills!

Wills and Estate Documents

Don't assume that only wealthy ancestors had wills or other estate documents, and don't assume the only thing you can learn from a will is just how wealthy that ancestor was. Quite a few people of more modest means chose to execute a *Last Will and Testament* to ensure what little they had remained with whomever they chose to leave it. Some seemed motivated by a chance to tell certain people things they never told them during life (such as how much they loved someone—or how much they loathed them) more than by the need to dispose of property.

These documents can often offer clues to family composition because children's names and ages were commonly mentioned, for example. Sometimes they might provide the first or only clues available as to the identity of some of the in-laws who married into the family. Wills from earlier centuries are especially important to researchers who had slaves among their ancestors (we'll talk more about special research problems like this later in the book).

But perhaps the most exciting thing about a will is that it may be the only existing written document an ancestor personally left behind. Depending on the ancestor, some wills can give us insight into what they were like as people: their personalities, how generous or miserly they were, and so on.

These kinds of documents are scattered all over the Web, so again, put your search caps on. Your best bet might be regional sites that sometimes contain collections of such data from various individuals of the area. Check with the USGenWeb site (*www.usgenweb.org*) and/or at RootsWeb (*www.rootsweb.com*) for the state and county your ancestor was from.

The following figure shows an example of the kind of information you might find.

A transcribed will from 1874.

Immigration and Naturalization

You may not need immigration or naturalization records early in your research, but chances are that you'll eventually want to use them. Since most people other than Native Americans descend from people who came to America from other countries, these records can be an important resource for clues to origin and other information. The most prevalent immigration records online are in the form of ships' passenger lists. Many of these records will show an immigrant's name and age, occupation, country of origin, race, and names of other family members. Some might include even more information.

Immigration records weren't required in the U.S. until 1820, so records prior to then might be harder to come by. You can learn more about immigration and naturalization records at the NARA site. They even have online samples of original records filed for surviving passengers of the ill-fated *Titanic* who arrived in New York City aboard the *Carpathia*. You'll also want to see the Immigrant Ships Transcribers Guild site at *istg.rootsweb.com* for online records transcribed by volunteer members of the Guild.

Passenger list for the Patrick Henry, *which arrived in New York in 1847.*

Court Records

Did you know that a wide variety of court records are available to the public? These range from minor civil court suits or divorces to real estate or probate records, and more. Public availability of any given type of court record may vary according to the locale in which it exists, and the type and amount of information provided will also vary widely. Volunteers constantly build the USGenWeb Archives Project (*www.rootsweb.com/~usgenweb*) to include more and more of these and other records.

Land Records and Deeds

Virtual Courthouses

If you don't mind paying a fee for the convenience of online access to a much larger number of public records, you could try a commercial service such as *www.knowx.com*.

If your ancestor left a will mentioning land or buildings among his property, you'll want to look up any land records or other real estate transactions you can find. If census records indicate your ancestor was a farmer or rancher, that's another good clue to seek out land records (though not all owned land, it's always worth checking). Again the USGenWeb Archives is a good resource for these types of records online. See the Alabama section at *www.rootsweb.com/~algwarch/land_deed.htm* for examples of records you might expect to find from this and other states.

If your ancestors lived east of the Mississippi River, you might be able to find copies of land records from the U.S. *Bureau of Land Management* (BLM), Eastern States, *General Land Office* (GLO). At their site, you'll find database and image access to more than two million federal land title records for the Eastern Public Land States issued between 1820 and 1908. Access is free, but you can also order certified copies of records for a fee. The site is located at *www.glorecords.blm.gov*.

The following figure shows the top portion of a Homestead Certificate I found for my great-great-grandfather from the BLM site. The document tells how many acres he obtained and where it was located. At the bottom, the certificate is dated the 30th of June in 1891. I found it interesting to see that someone had first misspelled his last name as *Stevens*, then crossed it out and entered *Stephens*.

An image of an 1891 Homestead Certificate obtained from the BLM site.

1. Once on the BLM site (*www.glorecords.blm.gov*), type your zip code into the small field on the left, then press Enter. (The zip code has nothing to do with the search; it's just for demographic purposes.)

2. Click on either the text link or the map graphic for the state you want (I used Alabama for my example). Next, type your ancestor's last name into the field marked Patentee Last Name (I used Stephens) and his first name in the one marked First (I used Joseph). Now click the Genealogical Search Results button.

3. You should see three results if you're using my example; you may get more or less for your own search. In my example, I knew the third guy wasn't mine because the date is too far back. The first two are in about the right date range, so I checked both.

4. After clicking on the first name, I found he wasn't my guy because my ancestor was never in south Alabama (Baldwin County). The second one was the right man; I still have relatives in the Marshall County, Alabama, area today. To see the image of the original document, scroll down and click on the View the Document link (you need an image viewer that can handle TIFF files).

▼ **Try It Yourself**

▲

Military Records

Even if you had no ancestors who served in a war, some of their close relatives probably did. Military service or pension records could contain information that will help to further identify the family of the ancestor you're looking for. Some military pension files contain a great deal of genealogical information, but even records that contain little or none shouldn't be overlooked because of their general historical value.

More and more military records are being provided online every day. In addition to resources you may have already found while practicing, you might get a head start on finding these records by checking the military resources section of Cyndi's List at *www.cyndislist.com/milres.htm*.

The following figure shows an example of one such military resource.

UNIT	MEN	UNIT	MEN
1st Michigan Infantry	1884	2nd Michigan Infantry	1828
3rd Michigan Infantry	2722	4th Michigan Infantry	2455
5th Michigan Infantry	1642	6th Michigan Infantry	2085
7th Michigan Infantry	1399	8th Michigan Infantry	1726
9th Michigan Infantry	2074	10th Michigan Infantry	1576
11th Michigan Infantry	2430	12th Michigan Infantry	2425
13th Michigan Infantry	2120	14th Michigan Infantry	1665
15th Michigan Infantry	2485	16th Michigan Infantry	2345
17th Michigan Infantry	1344	18th Michigan Infantry	1372
19th Michigan Infantry	1245	20th Michigan Infantry	1145
21st Michigan Infantry	1560	22nd Michigan Infantry	1767
23rd Michigan Infantry	1512	24th Michigan Infantry	2124
25th Michigan Infantry	1031	26th Michigan Infantry	1077
27th Michigan Infantry	1944	28th Michigan Infantry	998
29th Michigan Infantry	1130	30th Michigan Infantry	1001
1st Colored Infantry	1628	Stanton Guards	88
2nd. Vet. Res. Corps	197	Hancock's 1st Vet. Corps	145

The Bottom Line

You're well on your way to being much more efficient a hero than that guy in the movies! In addition to some possible surprises you might have learned in this chapter, you should know

- Some of the most common government and legal records needed for genealogical purposes, and some of the ways they can help you find your ancestors.

- The difference between primary and secondary records.

- How different types of records can be used to support each other and/or lead to additional evidence.

- That more and more official records are becoming available and accessible from the comfort of your home.

Workshop

Use the following workshop to help reinforce the knowledge you've gained in this lesson.

Q My grandfather's age on his death certificate would mean he was born in 1901, but his birth record shows 1899. Which is right?

A A birth certificate is likely to be more accurate, since it recorded the birth much closer to the event itself. The informant for the death certificate may have made an educated guess, which gives you only an estimate to go by.

Q I know my ancestor lived in the same county I'm in because I inherited the family home. Why can't I find him in census records?

A Remember that county boundaries sometimes changed, so your ancestor may have been recorded in another county's enumeration. Also, enumerators were human and errors sometimes happened; they may have misspelled the name or even omitted your ancestor from the record. Or maybe your ancestor was enumerated while visiting someone else's home.

Q I already have a copy of my great-uncle's death certificate, so do I really need the SSDI?

A Since you have a primary record for the death, looking him up in the SSDI might not be necessary, but remember that the more evidence you find to support other sources, the more accurate your information will be.

Quiz

Take the following quiz to see how much you've learned.

Questions

1. True or False: Primary records are always vital records.

2. Name at least three types of records commonly used in genealogical research.

3. True or False: Only people who had a Social Security Number will be listed in the SSDI.

4. True or False: Even if an ancestor wasn't rich, he or she might have left a will.

Answers

1. False. Though vital records are considered primary, not all primary records are vital records (for example, a will is a primary record of the disposition of property, but a will is not considered a vital record).

2. Vital records (birth, marriage, death), census, SSDI, state and territory death indexes, wills, immigration, court, land, and military records. (Did you think of others not named here?)

3. True. But remember that only those whose death was reported will be included.

4. True. Wealthier people may have left more wills behind, but many poorer folks did leave one.

CHAPTER 6

Going Beyond Official Records

You already know that official government records and legal records make the best evidence to document your ancestors' lives. But what if you simply can't find a birth certificate, no matter how hard you've tried? Or what if you don't know who you're looking for in the first place? Obviously, you'll need some extra clues to help find certain ancestors.

Sometimes, "unofficial" records such as the ones we'll discuss in this chapter might be the only kind available for an ancestor. Other times, they might be the first indication that a certain ancestor ever existed and will lead to finding more reliable documentation.

You might find other religious and secular records besides the ones you'll learn about here, but these are some of the most commonly found and used for genealogical purposes. Remember to use these kinds of documents as general clues first, then try to find official records to support what you find. If you simply can't find vital or other records to verify your data, sometimes all you can do is hope for the best (be sure to mention in your sources and notes that the information wasn't officially verified).

Church and Religious Records

Many religious groups and denominations keep records of their members and leaders, including births, marriages, and deaths. Some of these records might be even more detailed and accurate than vital records maintained by the government. However, as good they may be, don't accept them as primary sources unless they are from a time before official vital records were required.

What You'll Learn in This Chapter:

▶ That church and religious records are important to your research.

▶ Some of the kinds of secular records in which you may find clues.

▶ How to watch for clues in personal records.

Also, keep in mind that even if an ancestor wasn't particularly devout, he or she may still have been registered in some way with a local church.

By The Way

In this section we'll be dealing with Christian denominations. You'll learn about researching other religious and ethnic groups in Chapter 8, "Moving Through Common Research Barriers."

The amount of information available from religious records can vary widely, and the type depends on the theological and social importance of the records maintained according to each denomination.

Church records are often rich with information, but sometimes the biggest problem is determining an ancestor's religious affiliation. For lots of tips to help you find out, and for more information, see "Research in Church Records" from *The Source: A Guidebook of American Genealogy*, available online (free) from Ancestry.com at *www.ancestry.com/home/source/src124.htm*.

The following figure shows a portion of a chapter from this helpful online book.

Chapter 6 from The Source, by Richard W. Dougherty.

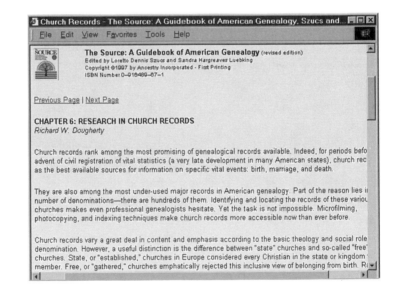

Church Hunting

Church records are scattered all over the Web, but you might start at RootsWeb (*www.rootsweb.com*) or USGenWeb for locations where your ancestors lived (*www.usgenweb.org*).

Parish Registers

Parish registers and similar records have been kept for hundreds of years. Parish priests were the official recorders of baptisms, marriages, and burials in areas where Roman Catholicism was the established faith. In 1614, parish registers were decreed obligatory by Pope Paul V.

The Church of England and the major Protestant denominations such as Lutherans and Calvinists also considered their priests and pastors to be official document keepers in areas where they were the established church or faith of the region. *Anabaptist* denominations (for example, Mennonites, Hutterites, Baptists) considered baptism—spiritual rebirth—more important than physical birth, so their records are more inclined to emphasize adult events rather than accurate birth records.

There are many, many more denominations since the early ones, but newer ones generally adapted the record-keeping practices of the earlier groups. Some of the types of church records you might expect to find are

Birth records

Baptism and christening records

Marriage records

Death and burial records

Confirmation records

Membership records

Minutes of the church council or vestry

Disciplinary records

Pew rentals or donations of funds

Family registers

Church Bulletins and Other Publications

If you think church bulletins are only good for reading about an upcoming sermon, the latest church supper announcement, or requests for donations, you might want to reconsider. Most also include births, weddings, deaths and burials, birthday and anniversary announcements, names of church members and staff, and sometimes more. Once I even saw detailed information in the form of a serialized church history.

Research Religiously

For some religious resources pertaining to genealogy, you might check *www.cyndislist.com/religion.htm.*

Some churches and denominational organizations also publish newsletters or magazines that contain information of historical and/or genealogical value. Many of these kinds of publications are available online, and some even provide archives of issues published in earlier times (see the following figure for an example).

Trinity Episcopal Church of West Virginia publishes a weekly online bulletin.

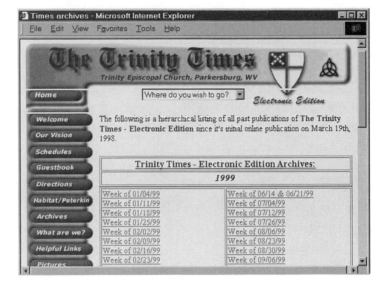

Cemetery Lists and Registries

In addition to records already mentioned, many churches maintain their own cemeteries and burial records associated with them. Some of these might be found online, but you're more likely to find simple lists of the interred or transcripts of headstone engravings from generous volunteers. These kinds of records can often be found on the different USGenWeb sites as well as on many personal genealogy sites.

Virtual Graveyards

The USGW Tombstone Transcription Project is a massive volunteer effort to catalog in one place online large numbers of cemeteries and the people who occupy them.

Not all cemeteries are affiliated with churches. You might find cemeteries and mausoleums maintained by local or federal governments, military branches, or individual families listed along with church cemeteries.

The following figure shows the Alabama index for the USGenWeb Tombstone Transcription Project (*www.rootsweb.com/~cemetery*); the other state indexes are arranged in a similar manner. To find specific cemeteries, click on the county name where your ancestor lived.

A good starting place for finding ancestral graves.

Just to let you know how helpful sites like this can be, while working on this book, I found a few of my ancestors' burial places about which I didn't know. I also relearned something I had forgotten—to not assume too much. I thought these folks were members of the Southern Baptist denomination, so I had previously overlooked the Methodist church cemetery in which they were interred. As Homer Simpson would say, "D'oh!"

▼ **Try It Yourself**

1. Go to *www.rootsweb.com/~cemetery* and click on the View The Registry link.

2. You'll be shown links to each state, so click on the state in which your ancestor was buried (I chose Florida). Now scroll down to your ancestor's county (Escambia County, in my example).

3. You may need to search through each cemetery listed for the county unless you already know where your ancestor was buried. I knew I should look in the Pensacola area, so I didn't have to check every cemetery listed. However, my example's correct cemetery turned out to be Latham Chapel Methodist Church in Barrineau Park, not in Pensacola.

▲

Miscellaneous Secular Records

Pulp Non-Fiction

When searching selected newspapers, look for items that might contain names, ages, births, graduations, marriages, divorces, deaths, burials, police reports, illnesses, and home addresses.

You're probably already familiar with many of the records we'll discuss in this section and the next, "Personal Records." Most are probably part of your everyday life to some degree or another, whether or not you ever give it any thought. Maybe you never realized that you might be surrounded by clues that can lead to solid genealogical information.

Newspapers

Most family scrapbooks include newspaper clippings in the collection of memorabilia, and for good reason. Newspapers have always been a great source for a diverse selection of information. Maybe you've seen clippings of Aunt Millie's wedding announcement or Grandpa Fred's obituary. Maybe someone in the family was given an award, or maybe someone else was involved in a crime story. If newspaper reporters and columnists didn't write about people, they would have very little to write about. Furthermore, each person mentioned in a newspaper is someone's relative! You can see how newspapers can be a rich resource for clues to historical and genealogical information.

Pulp, Part II

When searching selected newspapers, look for items that might mention out-of-town visitors (relatives), changes of residence, or any other information possibly relevant to your ancestor.

You can find specific newspapers online with various search techniques. You might even be able to find some reprints or transcripts online from some papers that no longer exist. Some existing papers provide archives of past issues or collections of certain features online. One place you might want to start looking for modern newspapers is the Newspaper Association of America (NAA) site at *www.naa.org/hotlinks*. There you'll find links to hundreds of U.S. and Canadian daily and weekly newspapers online. The following list might give you some ideas on the kinds of newspaper items in which to seek genealogical clues:

- Obituaries and burial announcements

- Wedding and birth announcements

- Society and community columns

- Hospital admissions and discharges

- News articles

School Records

Yearbooks and other records from primary and secondary schools or universities can give clues for further genealogical research. I've come across several collections of yearbook transcriptions during my Web travels, so you might want to try a search or two to see if you can find extra information this way. An interesting site you might also find helpful is ClassMates.com (*www.class-mates.com*). You must register to browse their listings of over two million (growing daily) U.S. and Canadian high school alumni, but the basic membership is free. If you choose, you can join with a paid subscription to access even more information. The following figure shows the site's main page.

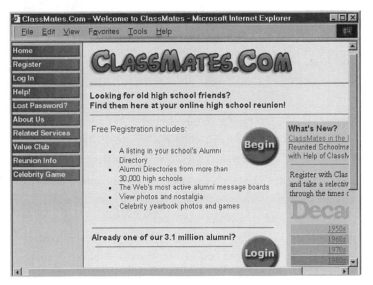

If you're curious, I'm a 1976 graduate of Walled Lake (Michigan) Western High.

Clubs, Lodges, and Other Organizations

Most clubs, lodges, fraternal organizations, and similar groups maintain membership rosters with varying amounts of historical and/or genealogical data. Some of these are more open with their past records than others. If your ancestor was known to have been a member of a local order or club of some kind, it could be worth trying to find their membership record. For an example of what you might expect, see the following page from the Independent Order of Odd Fellows (IOOF) that deals specifically with family history research: *www.ioof.org/IOOF/FamilyResearch.html* (shown in the following figure).

The Odd Fellows are good fellows for helping to find your ancestors.

Personal Records

You may physically have some of the records we'll discuss in this section. They may be boxed up and put away in your attic, or maybe they're at Grandma's house. Maybe personal records pertinent to your research are scattered among several relatives. Maybe you never thought of these personal items as genealogical or historical records before. If you're lucky, maybe a distant cousin or two has placed collections or individual records like these on his or her personal genealogy site.

Cause for Clues

Possibilities include diplomas, scrapbooks, baby books, greeting or memorial cards, employment records, insurance documents, report cards, awards, and citations.

Because of their personal nature, the kinds of records here will likely be found mostly on individual personal sites. However, many volunteer groups such as USGenWeb and others also offer online collections of transcripts, photos, and so on.

Family Bibles

Many family Bibles have been handed down through generations and contain invaluable data recorded by members of the family. Typically these include births, marriages, and deaths, but they may also contain other information such as personal notes, descriptions, and so on. Sometimes people don't realize the value of these heirlooms until too late, and there's no way to estimate how many family Bibles have been lost or destroyed over the years. On a positive note, more and more people are preserving these treasures and putting them online to share with others. If you have physical access to a family Bible, notice its copyright date and the handwriting that recorded family events. If all the entries appear to be the same color and in the same handwriting, or if the copyright is newer than any of the event dates, there's a good chance the events were recorded all at one time rather than as they happened. You can't count on this kind of record to be very accurate.

Photographs and Paintings

Images of ancestors not only add detail and personality to names and other data, but they can sometimes provide clues to further research. Clothing styles can help determine a period of time, for example, or an artist's or photographer's name on the front or back can sometimes be a clue to locations. Maybe there are shop signs, placards, or other details in the background that can also give you clues.

There are thousands of family photographs online among the many genealogy sites presented by families, volunteer groups, and commercial organizations. Additionally, you might find link lists like the "Lost & Found" section of Cyndi's List helpful (shown in the following figure). This page contains links to several sites that display ancestral photos waiting to find their rightful owners; you can find it at *www.cyndislist.com/photos.htm.*

Photos and docu-
ments wait to find
their true homes.

Cyndi's List – Photographs & Memories – Microsoft Internet Explorer

File   Edit   View   Favorites   Tools   Help

Lost & Found

- Ancestors' Lost & Found
  Dedicated to reuniting families with the memorabilia their ancestors left behind: photos, family Bibles, etc.
- Ancestral Photos
  Pictures found at auctions and in antique stores.
- AncesTree
  "The Family Tree with Photographs".
- "Fallen Leaves" Lost Leaves Photos
- Ford and Nagle
  Historians, Genealogists, and Collectors of Antique Family Photos, Family Bibles, and Family Documents
  - Antique Family Photos - A-C , D-G, H-Q, R-Z
  - Family Bibles
  - Family Documents
- Family Papers
  A service that helps family historians locate and own original documents pertaining to their ancestors.
- Granny's Lost & Found
  Lost: out of print books and films. Found: old photos, journals, documents, and letters.
- Lenore Frost's Dating Family Photos Homepage

The following figure shows a copy of a tintype that captured my great-great-grandparents for future generations to see. Though we're not absolutely sure, judging by the clothing styles, the romantic background, and the pose, we believe it was taken on or near their wedding day in 1867. I hope those somber faces were put on for the camera rather than a reflection of their feelings about the marriage!

My grandfather's
grandparents, ca.
1867.

Microsoft Photo Editor – elbridge&frances

File   Edit   View   Image   Effects   Window   Help

Letters, Postcards, and Address Books

Old letters and postcards can reveal much, including an ancestor's personality, sense of humor, and other personal traits. These extremely personal documents as well as address books and postmarked envelopes can also be valuable sources of historical and genealogical details. Like family photographs, transcripts (and sometimes scanned copies) of original letters and cards can be found on many kinds of genealogy sites, especially on personal sites.

The poignantly titled Letters From Forgotten Ancestors section of the TNGenWeb Project (Tennessee) provides some wonderful examples of letters written long ago. These contain joy and sorrow as well as names, dates, and much more. Who knows, maybe one of your ancestors wrote one of the letters at *www.tngenweb.usit.com/tnletters.*

The next figure shows the opening page of the Letters From Forgotten Ancestors project. Scroll down the page to click on the links that take you to the letter transcripts.

Margin Notes

Watch for an ancestor's notes in the front, back, or margin of a book, Bible, or pamphlet, on the back of an invoice, or on a scrap of paper.

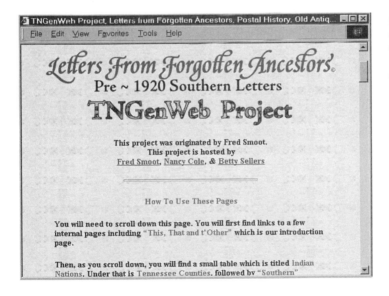

Letters From Forgotten Ancestors, a TNGenWeb project.

Diaries and Journals

My grandfather maintained a diary that contained pages and pages of short, rather boring entries like "Hot and dry this week" and

"Planted tomatoes." The entries were irregular; some were daily, and sometimes entire weeks were skipped. But every now and then, he wrote about big happenings—this relative had a baby, that one got baptized, or another passed away. He didn't provide great detail for these events, but it serves to show that even without being long, emotional, or colorful, an ancestor's dairy can still provide genealogical clues.

Many people have transcribed their ancestors' diaries, journals, and memoirs to present on the Web. As you search, keep in mind that even if you don't find the writings of your own ancestors, some events may be mentioned in someone else's diary or journal. Perhaps a neighbor recorded life and death events that happened in other nearby families as a sort of hobby, for example. If you're really lucky, you might find the diary of the neighborhood busybody where your ancestor lived!

Audio and Video Recordings

Family videos and sound recordings may be a bit hard to come by online, but I wanted to make sure to mention them so you won't overlook their potential. Members of your family may have old home movies on film or videotape, or perhaps someone has audiotapes of a relative telling stories. You never know what valuable clues these contain until you pay close attention to them (and take notes).

You might be interested in preserving your family history on audio or video recordings. You can find lots of resources online that will help get you started. You might pick up some ideas from the University of Kentucky's Oral History Program at *www.uky.edu/Libraries/Special/oral_history* (shown in the following figure).

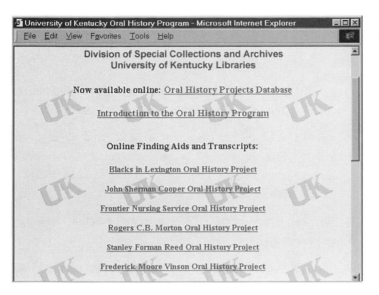

Get great ideas from past oral history projects.

The Bottom Line

You're on your way to a well-rounded research experience. In addition to some possible surprises you might have learned in this chapter, you should know

- That church records can sometimes be your best hope to help document your ancestors' lives.

- Several types of religious records you might find online.

- That newspapers as well as school and club records can give clues to find more data on individuals and families.

- That genealogical resources may surround you at home, and that you can also find many personal records online.

Workshop

Use the following workshop to help reinforce the knowledge you've gained in this lesson.

Q I heard that my great-grandfather never attended church. Is it worth looking for him in local church records?

A Yes, it's worth the search, especially if he lived when government vital records weren't yet required. He may have been a church member earlier in his life, and many churches kept records even on lapsed members.

Q How can a newspaper society column be helpful to my research?

A Such columns often provide names of local people who have parties, win awards, celebrate anniversaries, and so on. Some of those people might be your ancestors.

Q I saw an old photo online of a person with my surname, who bore a strong physical resemblance to my family. How can I tell if the person is one of my ancestors?

A Just because the person looks like you and shares your name doesn't automatically mean you're related, but you'll never know until you email the Webmaster and ask!

Quiz

Take the following quiz to see how much you've learned.

Questions

1. True or False: A baptismal record in a parish register is acceptable as a birth record.

2. Name at least three secular family history resources that might be easy to find either locally or online.

3. True or False: Lodges are too secretive about their membership records, so it's probably not worth researching.

4. True or False: Old letters and diaries are good sources of genealogical information.

Answers

1. False. Although the record might give a good clue to the person's birth date, it's not really a good substitute for a birth record unless it was before vital records were required by government.

2. Newspapers, school records, club or lodge membership records, family Bibles, photographs, letters, diaries, audio and video recordings. (Did you think of others not named here?)

3. False. Though some are more open than others, clubs, lodges, and other organizations are worth checking out for genealogical clues.

4. True. Even if your ancestors didn't keep diaries or write letters, someone else may have written about them.

CHAPTER 7

When You Find Information, Then What?

In Part I, "Laying the Groundwork," you learned why it's important to take notes, record your sources, and keep track of where you've been. Now that you've had a chance to see for yourself what kinds of information and data are actually available online, it's time to review some organizational ideas and put them to practical use.

Though I've used some real-life examples based on my research in previous chapters, I won't be doing that in this one. The examples in this chapter are based on real research methods, but all data used in them are fictitious and for purposes of illustration only. Any resemblance to real individuals (living or dead) or real sources is purely coincidental. Besides, I just wanted to have a little fun.

How to Handle What You Find

If you've been making notes and recording your findings as you practiced, good for you! If you haven't, well... there's never a better time to start (okay, you should have started sooner, but better now than later). If you use a genealogy software program, you've probably already printed out some forms to help you keep things organized, or maybe you found forms online to print and use. Or perhaps you even got creative and designed your own. We'll take a look at several examples of how you might handle what you find. If you've already developed a style of organization, that's great, but you might pick up some extra ideas along the way.

What You'll Learn in This Chapter:

▶ How to record what you found and cite sources correctly.

▶ How to verify your findings, and why this is important.

▶ How and why you should protect your work.

Recording Your Finds

As you learned earlier, forms for recording genealogical data can be very helpful for organizing your data. They can be found on several Web sites, or you can use forms produced by your genealogy software or that you designed yourself.

Be Creative!

Don't be afraid to experiment with making customized charts and forms. You might come up with some designs beautiful enough for gifts to family members.

If your genealogy program doesn't provide such forms (or if they don't meet your needs), take a look at the following examples. You don't necessarily need each of these kinds of forms; you can choose what works best for you. For most illustrations in this section, I used free forms downloaded from Ancestry.com (*ancestry.com*) and Genealogy Records Service (*genrecords.com*). Other forms may vary somewhat, but these might give you some ideas if you decide to design your own.

Note that most of the following forms are in PDF format; if you choose to download them, you need the Adobe Acrobat Reader® for viewing and printing (if you don't already have it, you can get it free at *www.adobe.com*). These forms are designed to be printed, then filled in by hand.

Try It Yourself ▼

1. If you don't yet have the free Adobe Acrobat Reader or if you want the newest version, go to *www.adobe.com*. To the right of your screen, look under Product Information and click on Free Tryouts & Betas.

2. You'll be shown a list of products; click on Acrobat Reader. Next, click on Select to Download the Full Version of Acrobat Reader.

3. Follow the simple step-by-step instructions to download and install the Reader. This page also contains links to further information, such as minimum system requirements, troubleshooting, and extra product information. Once you've finished, you'll be ready to view, print, and save a wide variety of documents found all over the Web.

▲

Family Group Sheets

The following figure shows the top portion of a family group record form from Ancestry.com. It has lots of fields to fill out, providing areas to record many major events in your ancestor's life.

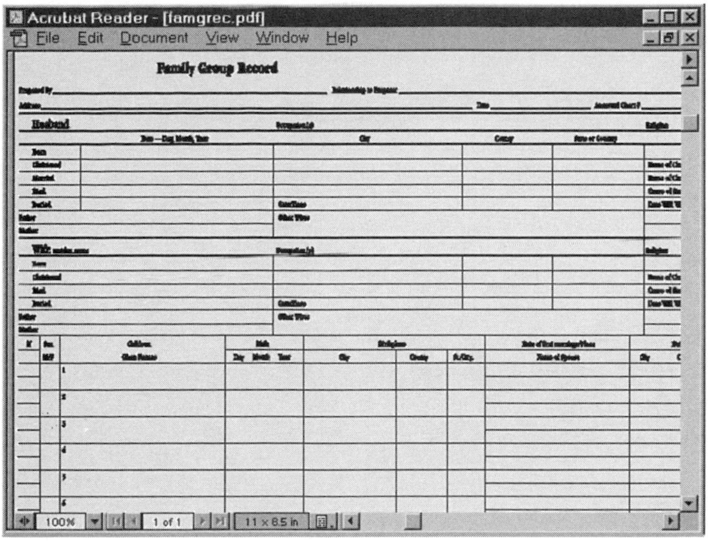

This family group sheet can record a wide variety of data.

The next figure shows the top portion of a family group sheet from Genealogy Records Service (GRS). This one also provides areas to record most major events, but data fields are larger so you won't have to write as small (the form will print two pages).

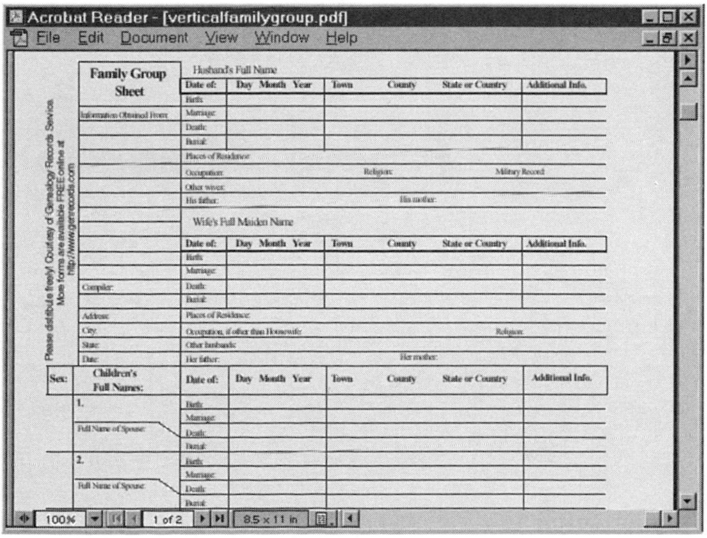

A two-page family group sheet with lots of data fields.

The following figure shows the top portion of a simple family group sheet you can make in your word processor or text editor.

*You can make
your own group
sheets in text file
format.*

```
W Microsoft Word - Family Group Sheet                          _ □ ×
 File  Edit  View  Insert  Format  Tools  Table  Window  Help        _ 8 ×
 L  . . . 1 . . . . . 2 . . . 3 . . . 4 . . . 5 . . . 6 . . . 7 . . .
    |                    Family Group Sheet #
    =========================================================
    Husband:
    Born:                    place:
    Marr:                    place:
    Died:                    place:
    Parents:
    Sources:
    =========================================================
    Wife:
    Born:                    place:
    Died:                    place:
    Parents:
    =========================================================
    CHILDREN
    =========================================================
    #1:
    Born:                    place:
    Marr:                    place:
    Died:                    place:
    Spouse:
    ---------------------------------------------------------
    #2:
    Born:                    place:
    Marr:                    place:
 Page 1    Sec 1      1/2    At 1"    Ln 1    Col 1   REC TRK EXT OVR WPH
```

You can use it to print blank forms or enter data directly onto the
sheet from your computer. You can add more data fields or fancier
formatting, but it shouldn't contain any less than the example
shows.

Ancestral (Pedigree) Charts

This figure shows a portion of an ancestral chart from
Ancestry.com.

*A simple but
effective ancestral
chart.*

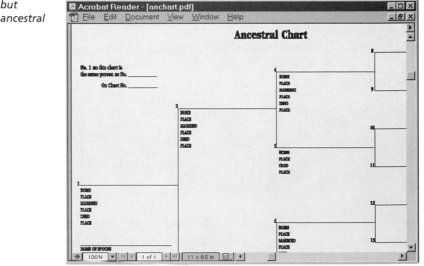

The next figure shows a portion of an ancestral chart from GRS. You'll notice that the previous chart is similar, but you may find one style easier to use than the other. Both charts allow up to four generations of data on one page (you'll continue the pedigree lines on subsequent charts).

If you're ambitious enough to design your own pedigree charts, you certainly have my blessing. I haven't personally attempted this, but with the variety of software available today, you can make almost anything!

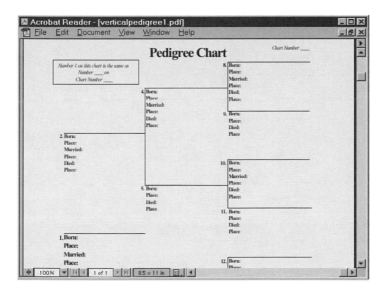

This ancestral chart provides keys to abbreviations.

Research Logs and Extracts

The following figure shows the top portion of a research calendar from Ancestry.com. This simple list format is a typical style for many research logs.

Adding and Abstracting

You can find census abstracts (forms to record census data) for every U.S. federal census year free to print from your Web browser at *www. familytreemaker.com/ 00000061.html*.

A simple research calendar in list format.

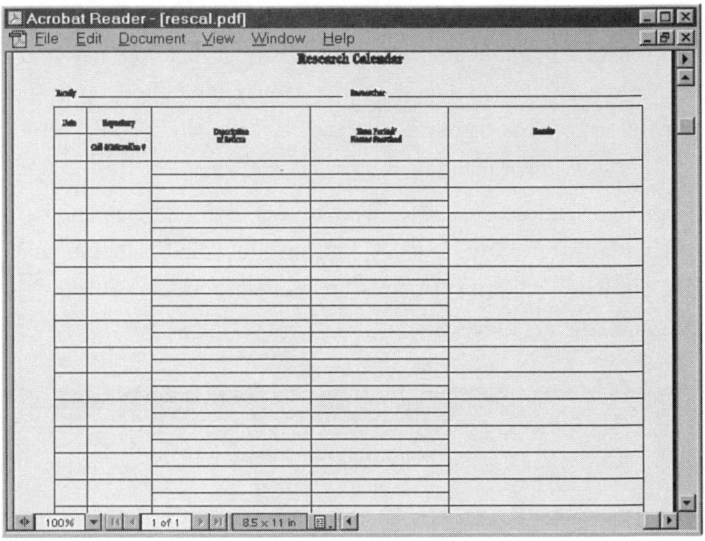

The next figure shows the top portion of a research extract form from Ancestry.com. This is similar to a research log, but it allows more details so that it actually becomes a way to record data as well as complete source citations. The format is somewhat like a library catalog card.

This research extract provides two "cards" per page.

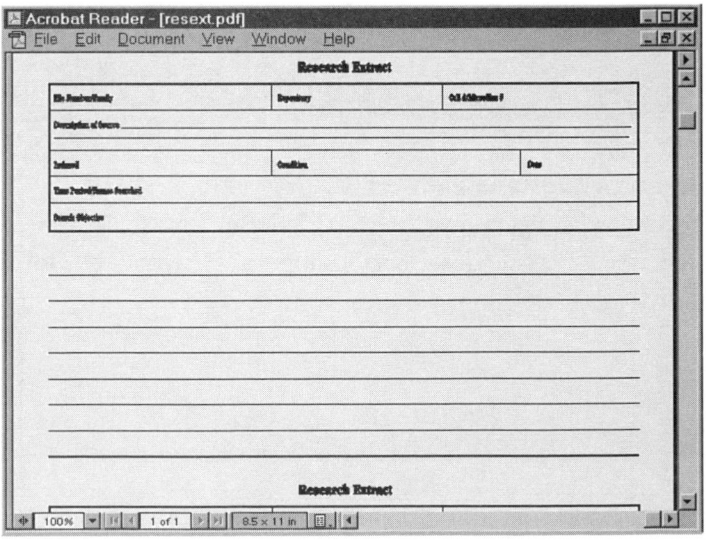

The next figure shows the top portion of a research log from GRS. The style is typical of many research logs, and this one offers larger fields for your entries.

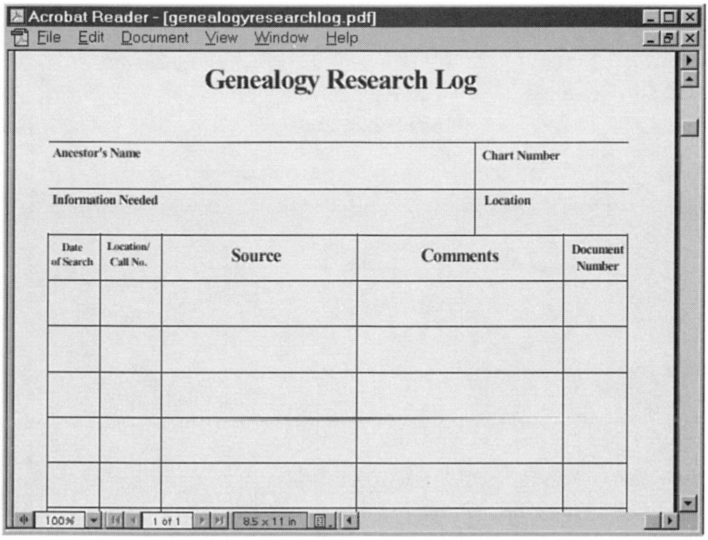

A simple research log with large fields in which to write.

The following figure shows the top portion of a cemetery log from GRS. This could be handy to take with you during a walk through a cemetery or to record data while at an online site with relevant grave listings.

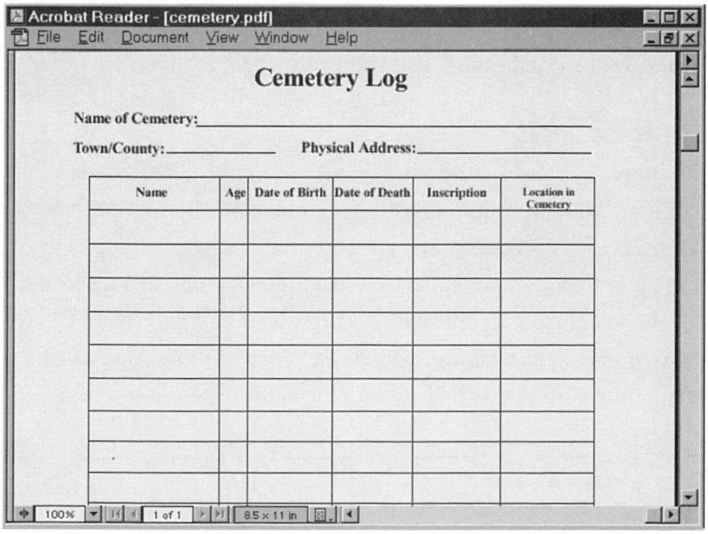

A simple but handy cemetery log with large data fields.

The following figure shows the top portion of a marriage log from GRS. Similar to a cemetery log, this could be handy to take with you while physically researching marriage records or to record data while at an online site with relevant data.

A simple but handy marriage log with large data fields.

If you prefer, you could create a variety of research logs yourself. In addition to the types in these examples, you might want to include other data-specific logs such as those for birth, death, or census research, or any of the variety of other kinds of records you find. If none of these examples strike your fancy, take a look on the Web to find others you might like better.

Citing Sources

Makin' Copies

It's a good idea to make photocopies of relevant pages from books and periodicals, including the flyleaf or other identifying pages.

You may get weary of hearing about the importance of source citations, but you might as well get used to it. If you think keeping meticulous records takes a lot of time, consider that it only takes a few moments to cite each source as you record each finding. If you neglect to cite your sources well and later want to go back to look at something, you'd likely spend more time to find it than you would if you had recorded it thoroughly in the first place.

If you're preparing a formal family history, there are no shortcuts; you *must* cite your sources thoroughly and correctly. Otherwise, how will you answer those who will inevitably ask, "How do you know this?"

If you use genealogy database software, you'll want to include your source citations along with your data. You might find it helpful to use printed forms or your word processor to collect your source notes and then enter them all at the same time into the software database.

Alternatively, you might want to try a method some genealogists use: Enter your citations into your genealogy database, then copy and paste the text to a word processor. Next, insert copies of matching records (a printout of a Web page, for example) into your printer in such a way as to print the citations directly on the backs of the documents. The citations match your database exactly, they won't be separated from the documents, and the process can save time.

Copy That?

It's a good idea to photocopy any records or postal correspondence you receive.

Following are some common genealogical sources and generally accepted formats for citing them. Remember to record dates in genealogical format (DD Mon YYYY), and for consistency, use last names first. It's also a good idea to include a line specifying the repository or archive where the source was found.

- **Interviews or anecdotes**. Person's name. Interview location, date. Example:

  Source: Bouquet, Violet. Her home at 123 Wildflower Lane, Gardenville, New Jersey, on 21 Jul 1997. Personal interview. (Recording "Aunt Vi at her house in the summer of '97" isn't enough.)

- **Books**. Author name. *Book title*. Publishing location: publisher, publication date. Page number(s). Example:

  Source: Abounds, Luna C. *Tornado Alley Survivors: Nebraska Families*. Corn City, Nebraska: Cornhusker Press, 1949. Page 69. Corn City Public Library, Nebraska. (You might also include the ISBN, edition number, and other details.)

- **Periodicals**. Author of article. "Article title." *Publication name*. Volume number, issue number: page number(s). Example:

  Source: Graves, Manny. "Local Humorous Headstones." *Lilly City Genealogy Club Musings*. Vol. VII, No. 2: 17-21. Lilly City Public Library, Ohio. (You might also include the ISSN and other details.)

- **Web sites**. Author name. "Title of Document." *Title of Web Site* (if the citation isn't from the main Web page). Version or file name or number (if applicable or known). Date on Web page or last revision date. Web site URL (date you accessed the site). Example:

  Dover, Matthew "Handy" and Goode, Stephanie Mae Dover. "GEDCOM Files from Our Family Tree." *Descendants of Kevin "Ben" Dover and Lorimae Smackett*. dover99.ged. 1 Apr 1999. http://www.doverfolks.com/gedcom.htm (30 Apr 1999). Internet. (You might also include authors' email addresses and other details.)

- **Records**. Record type/name and location. Book or file number, page or record number. Example:

  Source: Marriage license on file at Cotton County Courthouse, Cotton City, Alabama. Marriage Book G, page 99. (You should include microfilm number, call number, and other details appropriate to the actual record type and source.)

- **Correspondence**. Person's name (and online nickname, if any). Organization affiliation, if any. Email and/or postal address. Example:

Printer Workout

It's a good idea to print out copies of relevant Web pages and emails to include with your research records.

  Source: Kay, A. O. (Genielady). Fortune City Genealogy Club of Texas. hfuller@just4fun.com, 321 Happy Drive, Fortune City, Texas 54321. (You might also include phone numbers and other details.)

Verify What You Find

As you collect data, things might seem either scattered or all jumbled up at first, and you might even find some conflicting data from different sources. Now comes the part where you'll try to make sense of what you've found so far, and make sure it's as accurate as possible. This is where you'll find out how truly helpful it is to keep clear and accurate records (and if you didn't, you'll probably wish you had).

Getting It Together

I hope you've chosen a genealogy software title by now (if you didn't already have one), because it can make your genealogical life so much easier than compiling your own database either by hand or with software not designed specifically for genealogy. There's no way I can personally provide realistic reviews of all the genealogy software available (that would take another book or two!), but reviews by various software users are available online. You might choose to check out some of the titles listed in the "Software" section of Appendix A, "Recommended Sites."

Smooth and Simple

Genealogy software can help during verification. Everything is already in one place, and you can usually update or correct data automatically for all connected folks.

If you've already entered information for an individual into your database, you'll want to go through each of your records, notes, and logs to be sure you've included everything you have for that individual.

It's best to stick to one family line at a time, and work backward through the generations. You'll find that you've gathered a good deal of information on some individuals, and very little on others (ideally you'll have complete records for later generations first, then fill in the older ones as you research further). When you finally come to a person up the line for which you have no data, begin gathering and/or entering data for another family line. Remember to keep an eye open for further data on individuals you've already researched, even if you thought you were finished with them.

If you find conflicting information, make a note of it and recheck the appropriate sources. It could be that you simply mistyped something from one source or another. If the data truly does conflict, you'll need to look for more sources to determine which is correct.

Verify!

Don't consider your job done until you've verified as much information as possible for each individual that you've found. This means finding primary sources (especially vital records) wherever they exist. It's okay to enter preliminary research results or "guesstimates" into your database, but include notes to specify that the information is unverified. This might seem minor, but considering that soon you're likely to have scores of people in your family tree, without those comments, you could easily forget which data is verified and which isn't. Then you'd have to retrace your steps to be sure!

Protect Your Work

When first starting out with your research, you may overlook the need to ensure that nothing bad happens to your invaluable documents and mementos, the results of your hard work. It might not seem like that much in the early stages, and there's no fun in thinking about disasters. But anyone who thinks misfortune only happens to "someone else" might later find himself or herself presented with an unpleasant surprise. As "someone else," I can personally attest to how difficult it is to have worked so hard only to lose all my research materials because of an unexpected event. I'm still trying to recover from that loss, but I'm getting there!

Scare Tactics

Think like an insurance salesman when considering the value of your time and research materials: "Bad things happen, but don't wait until they do. Prepare against them now."

Your first line of defense against accidents, natural disasters, or intentional destruction of property is to make copies of all your important papers and share them with relatives and/or friends. Don't forget to regularly back up your important computer files, and keep copies of those away from your home, too. Antiques and original documents may require special care to preserve them well into the future. There are a variety of online resources to help you learn how, but you might enjoy the following page as you begin searching for more: *members.aol.com/lredtail/Kevins.html.*

The Bottom Line

While learning how to handle the information you find, you expanded on some of the concepts you learned earlier in the book. In addition to some possible surprises you might have learned in this chapter, you should know

- Correct ways to cite different common genealogical sources.

- About a variety of different types of forms you can use to record your findings.

- That using genealogy software can make it easier to catch and correct conflicting data as you verify what you found.

- That bad things can happen to good people, so it's important to protect your hard work.

Workshop

Use the following workshop to help reinforce the knowledge you've gained in this lesson.

Q I found data in a book excerpt that's on a Web page. Should I use the book as my source citation, or should I cite the Web page?

A Cite both. Use the Web site information first (since you didn't see the book yourself), then add the book citation. The Web author may or may not have given a complete citation, and you might want to inquire further.

Q I need family group sheets that include fields for LDS ordinances. Where can I find them?

A Many are available online, or you can obtain them from your local LDS Family History Center. Another option is making your own forms in whatever style suits you best.

Q I found a whole section of my family's data listed on a Web site. Why should I verify the information?

A The data may be accurate, but you won't be sure until you verify. Perhaps the Web author received his or her data from someone else, and that data may have passed through several other hands before then. That means a greater possibility of errors introduced along the way.

Quiz

Take the following quiz to see how much you've learned.

Questions

1. True or False: It isn't necessary to include microfilm roll numbers in source citations for census records.

2. Name at least three kinds of genealogy forms that might help keep your research organized.

3. True or False: You can't consider any research finished until you've verified all data.

4. True or False: It's important to make extra copies of documents and to back up computer files.

Answers

1. False. You should include as many details as possible in your source citations.

2. Family group sheets, ancestral charts, general research logs, research extracts, cemetery logs, marriage logs, census abstracts. (Did you think of others not named here?)

3. True. But even when you're "finished," be sure to stay alert for possible further information.

4. True. No one likes to think of bad things that might happen, but they can and do happen. It's better to be prepared in order to minimize possible losses.

PART IV

Where Do You Go from Here?

CHAPTER 8

Moving Through Common Research Barriers

If you're exceptionally lucky, you'll be able to research hundreds or even thousands of people in your family tree with no unusual problems. However, you're much more likely to encounter at least a few bumps in the road during your genealogical journey. In this chapter we'll discuss some common research problems (and a few not so common ones) that you might encounter, plus some ways to solve them.

Adoption

Perhaps one of an adoptee's hardest decisions might be choosing which family to research: his or her adopted family or the biological one. Let your reason(s) for wanting to trace your family tree in the first place guide your decision; it's a highly personal choice. Some adopted folks try to research both, but it's entirely up to you to decide whether you want to do so.

Whether or not your plans include a reunion with your birth family, you'll probably want to see the article "Search Basics for Beginners" at About.com's Adoption site (*adoption.about.com/library/weekly/aa062199.htm*). You'll find many other resources to help with your research from the same site, shown in the following figure.

What You'll Learn in This Chapter:

▶ What kinds of hurdles are presented by adoption issues, and where resources are that help you jump over them.

▶ Unique problems associated with researching certain ethnic groups and resources to help solve them.

▶ Why females can sometimes be hard to research and tips to help find them.

▶ Family skeletons and other potentially sensitive issues, and some ways you might handle them.

An amazing variety of adoption resources from just one site.

Reach Out

Free adoption registries can be found all over the Web. Register yourself or see if someone is seeking you or your relatives.

For a historical perspective—to become familiar with why some of the research problems unique to adoption exist—see the brief history of adoption at Texas Coalition for Adoption Reform & Education (TxCARE, at *www.visualimage.com/txcare/history.html*). For some clues to help find ancestors who were adopted, see the Orphan Train Collection presented by Orphan Train Heritage Society of America, Inc. (OTHSA) at *pda.republic.net/othsa*, shown in the next figure.

OTHSA shares memories and information about the infamous "orphan trains" begun in the 1850s.

Ethnic and Religious Groups

Your research on people within an ethnic or religious group
begins the same as any other (with yourself, working backward,
and using primary records whenever possible). However, there are
some research problems unique to different groups, so you may
need to stray a bit from the usual path or focus on certain
resources to obtain information required to complete your family
tree.

In this section we'll primarily discuss ethnic research, but you'll
also find resources to further your research within other religions
and cultures.

African Americans

Being a black American doesn't automatically mean you're a
descendant of slaves (historians estimate that at least one in ten
African Americans was already free when the U.S. Civil War
began in 1861). However, it *is* true for many, and genealogical
research for slave families can be complicated.

The biggest problem is the difficulty of finding records for many
of these ancestors. Loathsome as we find the concept today,
slaves were considered property rather than individuals. Thus,
there are fewer vital and other records available prior to the late
19th century. This means you'll need to research slave-owning
families in order to find information for the slave families themselves (owners' probate records and bills of sales might be needed
to find slaves' names and ages, for example).

Even if your ancestors were from a long line of free blacks, you
may encounter problems. Records for free blacks were not always
entered into the same ledgers or kept in the same locations as
those for Caucasians, even after political and social reforms
following the Civil War. Additionally, you may have surname
problems with ex-slaves before or after the war (probably especially true of runaways). Slaves didn't always keep the surnames
of former owners, even if they parted on good terms. Some did,
but upon gaining freedom, many former slaves adopted surnames
from earlier generations in their own families, and others adopted
names of unknown origin.

Helping Hands

Non-black families
can help African
American researchers
by sharing data
about slave-owner
ancestors. Many are
already doing this
online.

Thanks in part to Alex Haley's famous book and TV mini-series *Roots*, large numbers of people (of many heritages) have become interested in family history research. As a result, more and more African American research resources are becoming available online. Among these, one of the most comprehensive I've seen is Christine Charity's genealogy site (*www.ccharity.com*). The following figure shows an example of only a very small portion of the kind of content available on her site.

Here you'll find a wide variety of African American resources, Christine's own family history, and more.

Jewish Americans

Jewish heritage is considered both of an ethnic and a religious nature. After the destruction of the First and Second Temples in Jerusalem, Jews scattered as they migrated throughout the world (known as the *Diaspora*, Greek for dispersion).

Though they shared the same religion, many different cultures developed as the Jews settled different geographic areas of the world. Those who migrated to today's Central and Eastern Europe areas are known as *Ashkenazic Jews* (from *ashkenaz*, Hebrew for Germany). Those who settled the Iberian Peninsula are known as *Sephardic Jews* (from *sepharad*, Hebrew for Spain). There were other groups, but most Jewish Americans today descend from either Ashkenazic or Sephardic Jews.

Perhaps the main obstacles in Jewish heritage research stem from inconsistent surname practices and vital events recorded with minimal facts or not at all. Rabbinical pedigrees are an exception; details were meticulously recorded to document lineages of high honor. Even today, Jewish culture doesn't require hereditary surnames. In the Jewish religion, people are known by their religious given names, followed by *son of* or *daughter of* the father's given name.

Many did eventually adopt surnames by the 19th century due to religious persecution or governmental decrees. Some names were based on occupations, towns, or *patronymics* (surnames based on the father's name); others were assumed from Roman Catholic sponsors. The poor vital records are due to centuries of persecution, which often made it necessary to keep Jewish background—you guessed it—in the background.

Despite these roadblocks, help is available online in the form of Jewish heritage groups and other researchers who generously share their knowledge. One resource you might want to begin with is the *JewishGen Family Finder* (JGFF). This database contains thousands of surnames and towns submitted by over 25,000 Jewish genealogists worldwide. You can find the JGFF at *www.jewishgen.org/jgff* (see the following figure for an example of the site's main page).

Did You Know?
Anti-Semitism drove millions of Jews from Eastern Europe after Czar Alexander II was assassinated in 1881. Most Jewish Americans are their descendants.

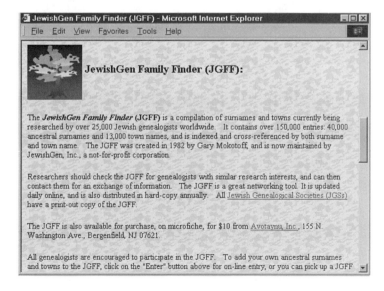

Search the JGFF database of Jewish ancestral towns and surnames, or you can add your own.

Latin (Hispanic) Americans

Hispanic immigration to the U.S. is much more extensive and began much longer ago than some might realize. The earliest Hispanic settlers in today's United States were in Florida (1565) and New Mexico (1598). Immigration hasn't stopped yet. People from Central and South America, Cuba, Mexico, Puerto Rico, and the Caribbean islands continue to come to the U.S.

Many might trace their roots through the Americas back to Spain, and others will find that their origins are actually African, Native American, or from European countries other than Spain (including Portugal, which is considered Hispanic by some). Central and South America have collected these cultures in a manner similar to the U.S. "melting pot."

The biggest problem for Hispanic researchers might be determining the actual location in the country of origin. The best approach (as with any other research) is to begin with what you already know and be thorough in working backward until you eventually find the mother country. You'll need to become familiar with specific emigration and immigration patterns to help narrow down the possibilities.

Church Clues

Most of your Hispanic ancestors were probably Catholic; don't forget the importance of church records.

Online Hispanic research resources are more sparse than some other groups, but more are becoming available as the Internet grows. One site you might want to check out is the AOL Hispanic Genealogy Special Interest Group (*users.aol.com/mrosado007*). You can see an example of their main page, which contains the group's charter statement, in the following figure.

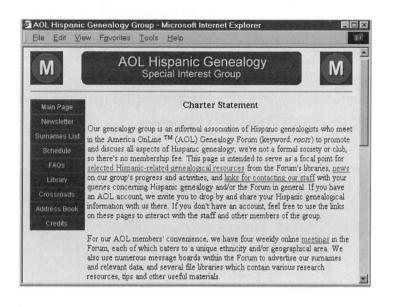

The Hispanic Genealogy SIG offers content, links to resources, and help from other researchers.

Native Americans

A large number of families have at least one legend that tells of at least one Native American ancestor. While this may be true for many, it's best to resist the temptation to assume you can trace your roots by beginning with an individual from a certain tribe down to your current generation. As always, begin with the present and move backward into the past.

Story People

Oral traditions are strong among Native American peoples, so you'll want to interview relatives as thoroughly as possible.

The greatest challenge will typically be due to the fact that Native American kinship terms and naming patterns were very different from European American traditions. For this reason (perhaps even more so than in other areas of your research), it's crucial to obtain a good working knowledge of general history and tribal traditions in order to fully understand Native American culture. You must place your research in a historical context to have a better chance of finding those ancestors.

Fortunately, interest in Native American heritage has never been greater, and there are many online resources for historical and genealogical research. For starters, you might like to check out the links in the Native American section of Cyndi's List (*www.cyndislist.com/native.htm*).

The following figure shows a portion of the Oklahoma/Indian Territory Project site, accessible from USGenWeb (*www.usgenweb.org*).

Links to tribal nations in the Oklahoma Territory might help find your Native American ancestors.

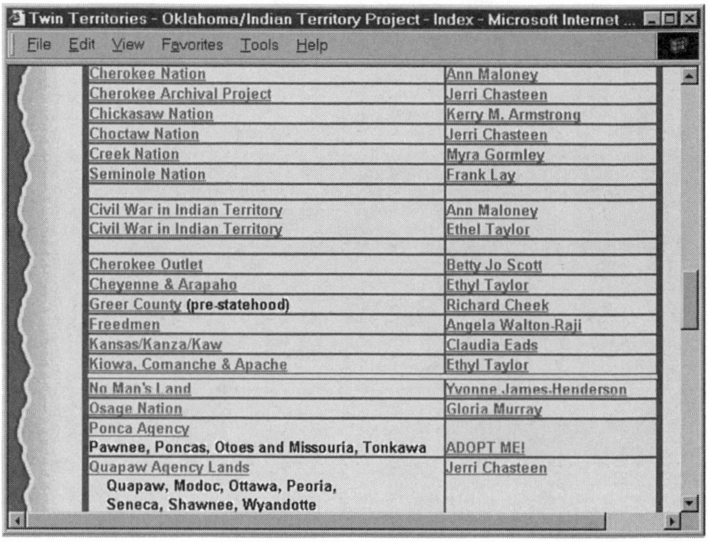

Other Groups

Though the following list is by no means all inclusive, it shows an example of the scope of ethic and religious groups (plus some other kinds of groups) for which you can find information and data online:

Acadians and Cajuns
The Amish
Asian Americans
The "Black Dutch"
Creoles
Doukhobors
Eastern religions
Gypsies
Hessians
Huguenots
Hutterites
Melungeons
Mennonites
Moravians (Unity of Brethren)
Palatines
Quakers
Shakers

One resource you might use to explore some of these groups is
www.greenapple.com/~cshart/chlinks.html, shown in the following figure.

Links to religious and denominational archives and information.

Females

There's an old joke in which a man is comically astounded to
learn that "according to these records, fully 50% of my ancestors
were women!" It's a humorous thought, but it's also a true fact—
even so-called test tube babies need a man to contribute sperm
and a woman to provide an egg. It seems such a shame that
females have so often been overlooked in published genealogies.

Ladies Can Be So Elusive

One can make a case that women in most parts of the world today
enjoy the same rights and privileges accorded to men, and in most
cases, the same respect. But it wasn't always that way. In earlier—even recent—times, women were often treated as lesser citizens or even as a kind of property, and as such, of little or no
particular importance in the grand scheme of things. In addition,
consider the tradition in many cultures in which the woman
changes her name at marriage. Those earlier ancestors might
have thought, "Why bother recording her maiden name? It's the
married name that's important."

History or Hers?

A good working knowledge of women's history is essential to your research of female ancestors.

As if to prove that point, certain legal rights were often taken from women when they married. With so many societal and legal traditions that held males in focus, you no doubt begin to get a hint of why lady ancestors can sometimes be so elusive!

Tips to Find Clues

You should use the resources and methods already discussed in this book, but here's one case that can illuminate how important it is to keep tabs on an ancestor's siblings and other relatives (even if their data seem insignificant at first). Those people may not be your direct ancestors, but they were your ancestor's relatives. The clues you find from them can mean the difference between an incomplete family history and the heroic act of rescuing your lost ladies from oblivion.

Who's That Girl?

Unusual first names can often be good clues when a maiden name isn't known.

For some great general women's history resources, you might want to start with *womenshistory.about.com* (an example of the main page is shown in the following figure). For more tips and insights into researching females, you might read online articles like "Female Ancestry" by Roseann R. Hogan, Ph.D. (*www.ancestry.com/magazine/articles/female.htm*). You can use your Web search skills to find even more resources and data for any females you feel have fallen from your family tree.

Women's History at About.com offers links, original content, and interaction with other people.

The next figure is from Susanne Behling's Notable Women Ancestors site at *www.rootsweb.com/~nwa*. As Ms. Behling points out, our ladies aren't all necessarily famous, but each is notable in some way.

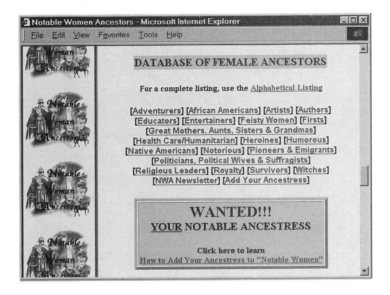

Browse the database of female ancestors, or add your own notable lady.

Sensitive Issues: Scandals and Such

Most of us are no doubt enlightened enough to realize that scandalous ancestors are not a reflection on modern generations. The purists among us will want to document all family history (past and present) as fully and accurately as possible, regardless of information we might find distasteful or sensitive.

Our goal is usually to document all the human frailties, strengths, failures, and successes our ancestors suffered and enjoyed. However, each of us probably knows at least one person in the family who would find some family matters offensive while we might find them amusing or simply as matters of fact.

For example, consider the matter of illegitimate births. While society doesn't necessarily condone premarital sex and pregnancy, unwed mothers today aren't usually the same targets of the hottest gossip in town as they were in earlier times. Researchers must face the fact that most families have had at least one case of illegitimate birth at some point in their history. And what about all those pirates, prostitutes, purloiners, gamblers, gunslingers, grouches, moochers, misers, and miscellaneous meanies of all sorts? They were all *somebody's* relatives, you know! (Take a gander at *homepages.rootsweb.com/~blksheep*, part of which is shown in the following figure.)

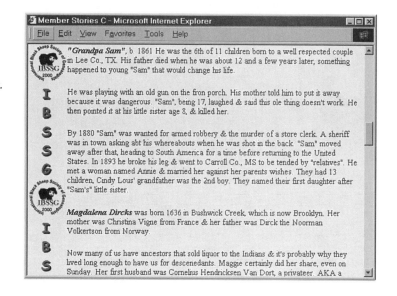

In addition to the usual kinds of "black sheep" in the family, you may encounter certain other information during your research that could present a potentially "sticky situation." For example, present and future researchers may find more same-sex marriages and/or transgendered individuals in their family trees.

Regardless of one's personal feelings on these situations, this kind of data is not handled well by any genealogy database software of which I'm currently aware. Your research may never include this type of information, but if it does, you might need to construct your own database in such a way as to properly record the names, dates, relationships, and so on.

A genealogist's problem isn't usually as much about finding potentially sensitive issues as deciding whether or how to present them to other family members. Some genealogists are so fearful of familial displeasure at the disclosure of certain facts that they become discouraged enough to stop their research. Others may share a watered-down or incomplete genealogy with their families just to prevent bad feelings (some even work twice as hard by maintaining two versions simultaneously—one public, and the other private).

Your choice for handling these kinds of issues is just that—yours. Only you know what's more important to you (to tell the whole truth and nothing but, or to fudge a bit on some of the more unsavory facts for the benefit of certain living relatives).

The Bottom Line

If you skipped to this chapter to learn about a group of special interest to you, be sure to review earlier chapters in order to develop a more solid basis for your research. In addition to some possible surprises you might have learned in this chapter, you should know

- Some of the complications presented by adoption issues, ethnic and religious groups, females, and scandals in family history research, and you've begun to find online resources to help.

- That many genealogy research problems stem from religious and cultural traditions or from historical acts of cruelty, persecution, and misunderstanding.

- That finding sensitive issues in your family tree is often the easy part; deciding how to share what you find with others in your family can sometimes present a bigger challenge.

Workshop

Use the following workshop to help reinforce the knowledge you've gained in this lesson.

Q Is it true I can apply for information about my birth parents from my adoption records?

A Yes, you can usually apply for non-identifying details from your adoption records. These do reveal some information about birth families, but not names. Details may vary depending on the specific repositories.

Q In my African American research, I came across someone referred to as *Estelusti*. What does that mean?

Ask Around

One way to get ideas to handle sensitive issues is to seek opinions of other researchers. Chat rooms, forums, and email groups are good places to ask.

A *Estelusti* refers to descendants of former slaves and freedmen who intermarried within the Native American Cherokee, Chickasaw, Choctaw, Creek, and Seminole nations. Learn more at *members.aol.com/angelaw859*.

Q **I found that one of my ancestors committed suicide after committing a terrible crime. Should I include this in my family history?**

A The short answer is that it's up to you. You might want to ask living relatives how they feel (they may not mind as much as you fear). Alternatively, you could include all the unpleasant details in your private or official version, and produce a more "sanitary" version for the family.

Quiz

Take the following quiz to see how much you've learned.

Questions

1. True or False: It doesn't matter whether you choose to research your adopted family or your birth family.

2. Name some reasons female ancestors might be hard to trace.

3. True or False: Most Jewish Americans descend from either Sephardic or Ashkenazic Jews.

4. True or False: Most modern genealogy software will handle unusual relationships well.

Answers

1. True. A more important point is to know why you want to trace either (or both); your reasons may influence your research focus and methods.

2. Society focused on males, females treated as lesser citizens or property, maiden names given up at marriage. (Did you think of others not named here?)

3. True. Additionally, the majority of Jewish Americans will ultimately find their roots in Eastern Europe.

4. False. As non-traditional relationships and roles grow in number, genealogy software will have some catching up to do.

CHAPTER 9

Filling In the Details

Remember when I said that the most common questions you'll ask during your research will be, "Who, where, and when?" In addition to those, you might want to ask, "What, why, and how?" The answers to these extra questions can help you compile a richer and more colorful family history by filling in the details that bring your ancestors to virtual life. If you find yourself facing a brick wall in your research, these questions may actually be necessary to help you find the clues you need to get past that wall.

In this chapter you'll learn some ways to get answers to some of your extra questions. For example, you might want to find out *what* your ancestors did for a living, *why* they moved from place to place, or *how* members of the family were affected by certain historical events. You'll also learn some basics about research in your ancestors' countries of origin after you've found your first immigrants to America.

What You'll Learn in This Chapter:

▶ How to bring ancestors to virtual life by learning about historical and everyday events that affected them.

▶ How learning about old customs and styles can enhance your research and help solve mysteries.

▶ How to begin researching outside America once you've found your first immigrants.

Ancestors' Daily Lives

What did your great-grandparents wear? What kinds of foods made up a typical meal for them? Did they have strong political, religious, or social views? What kinds of prices did they pay for goods and services? What did they do for fun? These are just a few of the questions you might find answers to not only by researching your ancestors themselves, but also by seeking out historical information about the times in which they lived.

Among the many historical resources available online, I'll bet a dollar—if I were wealthy I'd bet more—that you'll enjoy the U.S. Library of Congress site (the following figure shows the opening screen at *www.loc.gov*). One part you won't want to miss is the American Memory section (*memory.loc.gov/ammem/ammemhome.html*). There you'll find online collections of biographies, oral histories, photos, and much more. These collections contain items from around the world in addition to uniquely American memorabilia.

The Library of Congress site holds a treasure chest of historical gems.

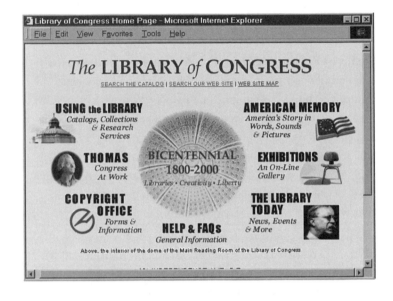

Historical Events

History Online

Two great sites for general history resources are *thehistorynet.com* and *historyplace.com*.

So far in my life I've witnessed major historic American events like nine different presidential administrations, the assassinations of several national heroes, the struggles of the Civil Rights Movement, military action in Vietnam, man's first step on the moon, and other advances and inventions that were once considered science fiction. There were many more, not even counting worldwide historical events, such as the rise of the Berlin Wall and the day it finally fell.

Just as we today watch history make itself, so did our ancestors. How did they feel about the politics of their times? What issues were important to them? What events touched them directly or indirectly, and how were their lives influenced?

Even if you can't answer for an ancestor's personal feelings, you can learn about past social, political, and religious attitudes in general with a little research. Sometimes this might be used primarily to flesh out your family history by making those ancestors more real to you. Other times, the information might provide good clues or insight into why they did certain things. For instance, you might learn why an ancestor moved from one place to another (or get a better idea of where); why he took a certain job (or what the job was); or gain clues to the cause of his death (important if you have medical reasons for tracing your family history).

Big Events

If your ancestor seems to have vanished without a trace, he or she might have been killed during a natural disaster (one as famous as the 1906 San Francisco earthquake or a lesser-known event), or maybe he or she died from illness during an epidemic. When large numbers of people died in a short period of time, some individuals might have been overlooked when the events were recorded.

Perhaps your ancestor joined others as they left an affected area in search of a healthier place to live, or the political or economic climate might have prompted a mass migration. Another possibility might be religious persecution or antisocial behavior toward certain groups. If people were distressed enough to suddenly move away, it seems reasonable that record keeping might have been the least of their worries at the time.

One resource to find which major historical events occurred on specific dates is Leon's Political Almanac at *www.magnolia.net/~leonf/cgi/hypercal.cgi* (the following figure shows a sample of what happened on 27 July in various years). For dates of major disease epidemics since 480 B.C., try the chronological list from Duke University at *www.botany.duke.edu/microbe/chrono.htm*.

On the Lam

Don't overlook the possibility that an ancestor may have fled the area after being accused of a crime, whether guilty or not. Check local news of the times.

*Historical political
events for 27 July
in various years.*

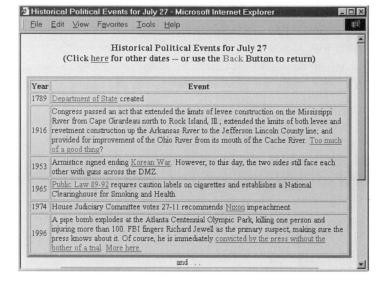

Historical political events for 27 July in various years.

Earlier Attitudes

Timely Clues

For quick historical references, search the Web for—and use—specific kinds of timelines (inventions, military battles, political events, medical advances, industry, and so on).

For some wonderful glimpses into contemporary attitudes of earlier times, check out the online American Life Histories collection from the Library of Congress site (the figure that follows shows the collection's main page at *memory.loc.gov/ammem/ wpaintro/wpahome.html*). There you'll find dialogues and narratives from hundreds of people who were part of the WPA Folklore Project from 1936–1940. The subject matter varies widely (recollections of slave life and other 19th century events to thoughts on the Great Depression, and more). These documents can offer a great deal of insight into our ancestors' lives.

For other general and specialized historical resources, try About.com's history section at *home.about.com/education/history* or use your Web search skills to find items of particular interest.

Historical Trivia

When I was a toddler I had a toy monkey named Khrushchev, after Soviet Secretary General Nikita Khrushchev (see the following figure). My father had named my little monkey friend; later I realized that it was really a subtle political statement. An innocuous bit of information can sometimes reveal a larger view.

Historical research would show that my toy with its unusual name reflected how many Americans felt during the mid-20th century—the fear of conflict involving nuclear weapons was often masked by humor. Not every tiny detail of your ancestor's life will be especially significant, but a good detective won't overlook the little things.

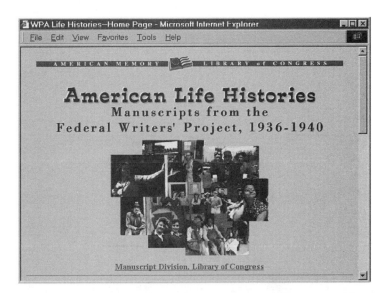

American Life Histories: thousands of memories online.

My techno-whimsical version of a childhood history lesson.

Work and Play

Work itself isn't trivial, but many occupations no longer exist, or a job's name might be different today. In that sense, obsolete occupations might be considered historical trivia, and you can find lists of them on various Web sites. For example, you might know that a *cartwright* was a maker of carts and wagons, but do you know what a *cod placer* was? This was a person who handled the fireproof containers that held pottery to be fired in a kiln. If your ancestor had an unfamiliar job title, you might find a list of occupations and their descriptions helpful (for examples, see *cpcug.org/user/jlacombe/terms.html,* shown in the following figure).

If you don't know the difference between an acaterer and a zincographer, sites like this can help.

The things that entertained your ancestor might provide clues to time periods, locations, or other information. For example, suppose an ancestor lived in the 1800s, but you don't know exactly when. You know he passed down the lyrics of a favorite contemporary song, but you don't know when or by whom the song was written. You might find clues from the Kingwood College Library site, where you can explore American Popular Music Before 1900 (*www.nhmccd.edu/contracts/lrc/kc/music-1.html,* shown in the next figure).

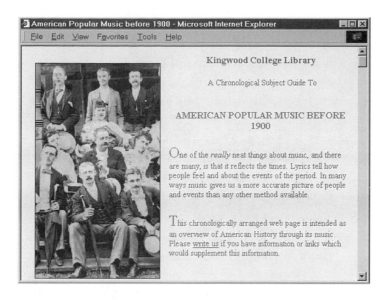

An overview of American history through music.

The following figure shows the main page of an online baseball card collection from 1887–1914 at the U.S. Library of Congress site. Not only is baseball still a favorite (both as player and spectator), but collecting the game's memorabilia is a very popular hobby today. Perhaps it seems remarkable that a simple marketing idea (baseball cards in candy and tobacco product packages) became a source of historical documents, but it did. The Web is rich with all kinds of historical information on art, music, dance, games, and many other pastimes. What did *your* ancestors do for fun?

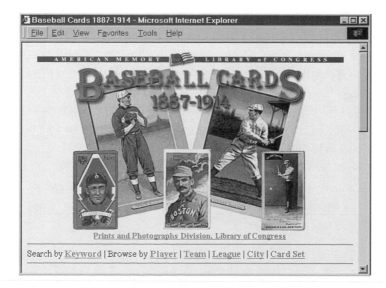

Baseball cards: an integral part of popular American culture.

Food and Drink

Email Fun

Trade folklore, humor, recipes, stories, traditions, and more with other researchers on the HOMESPUN-L mailing list (from *rootsweb.com*).

In the movie *Avalon*, the character Sam Krichinsky tells any child who will listen about how he came to America in 1914, and he tells stories about other events and people in his past, too. Much of the film is centered around family gatherings, especially holiday meals. During a traditional Thanksgiving dinner, some family members ask why they must hear the same stories so often, to which Sam replies that "If we don't remember, we forget." That happens to be my favorite line from the movie; it's a deceptively simple remark, yet it makes a profound statement.

Family Films

You might enjoy (and gain insight from) dramas and documentaries that highlight family traditions. You can even purchase them online.

Though many things have changed in our fast-paced world, holiday gatherings and family reunions are often still rich with traditions (favorite recipes or oral histories told by people like Sam Krichinsky, for example). Many of these stem from cultural, religious, or social customs of earlier times, and lots of family historians have shared theirs online. One place to find some of these is from the Recipes, Cookbooks, and Family Traditions section of Cyndi's List (*www.cyndislist.com/recipes.htm*).

Old Styles and Customs

Learning about the customs, styles, and fashions of earlier times might help clarify data already found or fill gaps in information. Sometimes you may find leads to further clues or add "personalizing" details to your family history.

Handwriting and Terminology

Learning about old handwriting and abbreviation styles isn't merely an interesting historical exercise; sometimes it's necessary to decipher the information on old documents. The same is true for old terms and phrases. An old death record may use an obsolete disease name as cause of death, and you want to know what it means. Perhaps old letters or diaries contain phrases with which you're not familiar, or you want to know what certain odd-looking abbreviations on some records mean.

Fun with Fonts

Experiment with different word processor fonts for possible clues to what handwritten mystery words might be.

There are many online resources for learning about these old styles and terms. The following list shows just a few sites from which you can learn more:

- Abbreviations Found in Genealogy,
  www.rootsweb.com/~rigenweb/abbrev.html

- AmeriSpeak: Expressions of our American ancestors,
  www.rootsweb.com/~genepool/amerispeak.htm (the figure
  following this list shows a small portion of this site's
  main page)

- Glossary of illnesses you might find during genealogical
  research, *www.rootsweb.com/~ote/disease.htm*

- Old handwriting and abbreviations,
  www.firstct.com/fv/oldhand.html

- Old lettering styles in handwriting,
  www.rootsweb.com/~ote/writing.htm

*AmeriSpeak helps
find the meanings
of old and collo-
quial sayings.*

Clothing and Other Fashions

Learning about clothing, architecture, furniture, or social enter-
tainment from earlier times might help with details in old pictures
or other documents, or you may just want to know more about
how your ancestors lived. You can use many of the online
resources we've already discussed to learn about these, or you can
search the Web for other information of particular interest
to you.

One example of an online resource that can provide insight into your ancestors' lives is a book called *A Belle of the Fifties* by Virginia Clay-Clopton (subtitled *Memoirs of Mrs. Clay, of Alabama, Covering Social and Political Life in Washington and the South, 1853-66*). Beginning with sketches of her childhood in the early 1800s, Mrs. Clay goes on to relate her experiences as the wife of politician Clement C. Clay, Jr.

Books Online

Project Gutenberg (*promo.net/pg*) has thousands of free e-texts you can read with your computer.

The narrative includes political and social attitudes, plus many details about food, clothing, and other styles and fashions of the times. You can read this 1905 book in its entirety on the University of North Carolina site at *metalab.unc.edu/docsouth/clay/clay.html*. There are other books on the Web similar to this one; you might even find one about your own ancestor.

The following figure shows a portrait of the book's author as seen on the UNC site.

Mrs. Virginia Clay-Clopton in a portrait from her book.

Researching Outside America

Ins and Outs

A reminder: to *emigrate* is to go out; to *immigrate* is to come in.

When you've found your first immigrants, you'll probably want to begin researching further by finding resources in the country of origin. In some cases, you may find an ancestor who left America to live in another country, so you'll want research resources for that country. There isn't sufficient space in this book to cover research outside America in detail, but I don't want you to think you have to stop at American borders!

Your First Immigrants

Before you "go back to the old sod" (even virtually), you'll need to know who your first immigrants were. Next, you must know when and how they came to America, and from where they came (you need at least the country of origin; you can research further to find the actual location within that country). Earlier in the book we discussed some resources for finding this information—ship passenger lists, naturalization records, and so on—and hopefully you'll use your search skills to find even more.

Resources from the Motherland

The types of records available from other countries vary greatly; this is true for both online and physical documents. Some countries offer much more official government data online than does the U.S., and some offer little or none. Different countries also have different methods of record keeping.

Sometimes you'll need to substitute other information in place of records that were previously lost or destroyed. One example of this is using the famous Griffith's Valuation—Irish land records— as a substitute for destroyed 19th century Irish census records. It isn't perfect, but it's better than nothing!

The number of worldwide genealogical resources online is growing all the time. One great place to start is with WorldGenWeb (*www.worldgenweb.org*). The following figure shows a portion of the main page. There are fifteen major world regions to choose from, then you can follow links to genealogy sites for different countries and sub-regions.

Take a virtual research trip all over the world with WorldGenWeb.

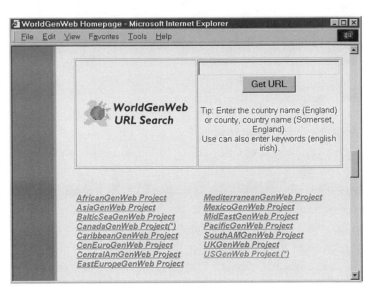

Try It Yourself ▼

1. Suppose you found your ancestor's name on a ship passenger list and Ireland was given as his country of origin. Go to *www.worldgenweb.org* and scroll down until you get to the Regional Index.

2. Click on the BritishIslesGenWeb Project link, and once you're there, scroll down to the Projects section. Now click on the Ireland link.

3. Now that you've arrived at the IrelandGenWeb Project site (shown on the next page), you can take your virtual genealogical research trip at your leisure. As you explore, you'll find places to post queries, resources for finding even more information, and tips specifically for tracing your Irish roots.

▲

The Bottom Line

If you skipped to this chapter to learn more about an aspect of extra research that especially interests you, be sure to review earlier chapters in order to develop a solid basis for all of your research. In addition to some possible surprises you might have learned in this chapter, you should know

• How to use general and specific historical resources to help and enhance your research.

- How to watch for seemingly trivial information that could lead to bigger clues.

- How old handwriting styles, obsolete terminology, and earlier fashions and traditions can help fill in gaps and lead to other clues.

- How you can take worldwide virtual research trips by using the Internet.

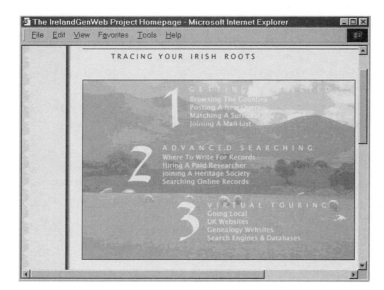

Tracing your Irish ancestry might be almost as easy as 1-2-3.

Workshop

Use the following workshop to help reinforce the knowledge you've gained in this lesson.

Q I noticed that an unusually high number of individuals in my family tree died between 1917 and 1919. What could that mean?

A There's a good possibility that they were victims of the famous influenza epidemic that peaked in 1918. You can use online resources to help determine whether this is the case.

Q While looking through census records, I saw *Jno* written where a first name should be. What on earth could that stand for?

A The abbreviation was most likely to designate the name John. You can find lists of these kinds of old (and sometimes odd) shortcuts on the Web. (You'll also find definitions for terms like this one in the Glossary.)

Q **I think my family name is Scottish. How can I find out where our first ancestors lived in Scotland?**

A Don't forget the first rule of genealogy: Start with what you know and work backward through the generations. When you know for sure your first immigrant was from Scotland, then (and only then) should you seek research resources for that country.

Quiz

Take the following quiz to see how much you've learned.

Questions

1. True or False: You can't really learn much about an ancestor's way of life unless he left lots of letters and diaries.

2. Name some possible reasons an ancestor may appear to have suddenly vanished.

3. True or False: A *fear-nothing maker* was a weaver of a special kind of thick woolen cloth known as *fear-nought*. (Hint: Use a Web resource mentioned in this chapter to help you find the answer.)

4. True or False: All countries outside America have the same kinds of records, and most of them are online.

Answers

1. False. You may or may not find personal details, but historical research can provide excellent clues as to what his life was like.

2. Wartime activities or an epidemic illness ending in death, adverse political climate, poor economic conditions, religious persecution, social ostracization, destructive natural disaster. (Did you think of others not named here?)

3. True. You can find descriptions of this and other old occupations online.

4. False. There is no certain standard. You'll find a wide variety
   between one country and any other as to the types and
   amount of data generally available online.

CHAPTER 10

Putting Your Family Tree Online

Once your family tree has a solid start and is growing steadily, you may want to put it online. Perhaps your primary interest is to share your findings with your own family, or you may want to build a Web site geared more toward exchanging further data with other researchers. As your research progresses, you might even want to share your experiences or provide education and tips for folks just beginning their own research.

If you've built a personal Web site before, you'll have no problem constructing a genealogy site. Even if you have no clue how to begin, take heart. It's not only possible to create an attractive and informative site, it can be much easier than you might think! In this chapter you'll learn some ways to get your family tree online and some important issues you need to know about before you get started.

Plan Your Presentation

Look at any successful construction project and you'll most likely find a set of blueprints somewhere. Just like an architect or a carpenter, you need to follow a plan in order to construct a successful genealogy Web site. Planning ahead will help prevent frustration and other problems later. The following steps can be a good basic guide. You might add extra steps, but even if you're an experienced Web builder it's important that you don't skip any of those I've listed here.

What You'll Learn in This Chapter:

▶ Some common legal and ethical issues to be aware of before you publish your data on the Web.

▶ How to protect your family's privacy and still offer lots of information.

▶ How to build a personal genealogy Web site.

Surf for Ideas

As you surf the Web, look for sites that might give you good ideas for your own site.

1. Make a checklist on which you should include (at minimum): a main page on which you describe what's available and (if more than one page) an index of links to other parts of your site; a list of the main surnames you're researching; the date of your latest site modification; your name and email address. Add other elements to the list as your situation indicates.

2. Make a simple storyboard or flow chart based on your checklist (see the example shown in the following figure). Decide exactly what to include on your site (group sheets? charts? photos? stories?) and in what order and style you'd like to present your material. This needn't be in great detail; you want something that can be easily modified if you change your mind.

Tom Christensen shows how to plan your site at HTML Wizards.

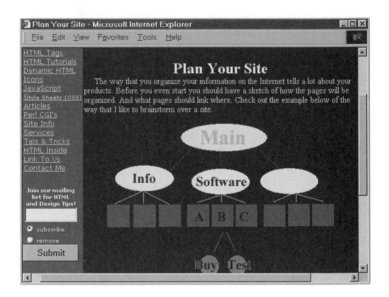

3. Choose creative titles for your site and each page on it. These should be brief but more informative than "Joe's Genealogy Home Page" (try "Kentucky Ancestors of Joseph Smith" instead). Generic titles don't reveal much about your site, and many won't bother to click a link to find out more about it.

4. Weed out potential problems. Read the next section ("Legal and Ethical Issues"). Be sure your material violates no copyright or trademark laws and that your presentation will be appropriate to publish online.

5. Put your plan into action. Read the section titled "Build a Genealogy Web Site." You might want to print out your particular plan for reference as you enter the construction zone for your new site.

6. Advertise! When your site is finally live online, people won't know it's there unless you tell them. Do this by word of mouth and email, and register your site with a variety of search engines and directories.

Legal and Ethical Issues

If you think it's okay to skip this section because you're a decent, law-abiding citizen, you might later find yourself wishing you had paid more attention. It's true that the majority of folks who publish personal Web sites are good people with no plans to break any laws or to exhibit unethical behavior.

The problem is that most folks new to Web site publishing (and some who consider themselves veterans) don't truly understand all that this can entail. But you, dear reader, are smart enough to plan ahead! Your plan includes learning how to avoid some common legal and ethical pitfalls before you start building your site.

Common Myths and Facts You Should Know

The word *publish* might be the most commonly misunderstood concept by folks new to building personal Web sites. When you think of publishing, you no doubt think of books (like this one), magazines, or other physically printed material. Many think of publishing only within a commercial context.

The truth is that "to publish" simply means to make something public, regardless of the media used or the motivation to do so. When you post messages to online forums or chat rooms, you're publishing. Even when you send an email, you're publishing (you have no control over where your recipient might forward it later). And yes, when you put your Web site online, you're publishing.

Now that you know what publishing really means, ask yourself a few questions. Would you announce all your family's intimate secrets in an auditorium filled with people? Would you stand up and recite a personal letter without first gaining the author's

Keep It Simple

Resist the temptation to attempt a large and fancy site on your first try. You can always add more later.

Avoid the Obvious

Titles don't need "Web Site" or "Home Page" added. They're already implied, and you'll have briefer, more descriptive titles.

permission? Would you rent a billboard and put someone else's material on it without permission? Chances are that you'd do none of those things. The Web addresses a much larger public audience than any auditorium or billboard ever could, so these questions (and your answers) are important to remember as you create your site.

Copyrights and Trademarks

Did You Know?

Facts can't be copyrighted, but the way they're presented can be.

Of the many misconceptions aboutcopyrights and trademarks that exist, I've heard the following ones most often—sometimes even from experienced genealogy folks.

- "It's okay to use copyrighted or trademarked material as long as you don't plan to make money from it."

- "It's okay to use copyrighted material as long as you credit the author."

- "If it doesn't have a copyright notice, it's not legally copyrighted, and is therefore considered public domain."

Did You Know?

After material has been placed in the public domain, it can't be copyrighted by anyone.

All three statements are *quite wrong*, but these myths and more are surprisingly widespread, considering that correct information can easily be found. Copyright and trademark infringement is a serious legal issue that even the best citizens might commit (usually by accident), so don't be misinformed!

Brad Templeton's "10 Big Myths" (*www.templetons.com/brad/ copymyths.html*) is fun and easy to read; a good article for quick reference. Stanford University's "Copyright & Fair Use" (*fairuse.stanford.edu*) can lead you to just about anything else you

Did You Know?

Just because a book is old, that doesn't automatically mean it's no longer under copyright.

want to know about copyrights and trademarks. Michael Goad's "U.S. Copyright and Genealogy" is geared specifically toward genealogists. The following figure shows a portion of his site at *www.rootsweb.com/~mikegoad/copyright.htm*.

Mike Goad takes on legal issues relating to genealogy.

Internet Privacy

During my two years as the About.com Guide for Genealogy, I heard from many people concerned about personal privacy online. One woman told of an incident in which she shared (in good faith) her private research data with a distant cousin whom she'd "met" online. She later found that he had submitted her data "as is" to a major software company for inclusion in a genealogy data CD product.

This lady was outraged that her work was represented as belonging to someone else, but that wasn't all. The cousin didn't omit data for living individuals. This caused concern for personal security and safety in my emailer's immediate family, especially for her minor children.

A few cases were even more extreme, and other situations might never cause any problems at all. However, privacy is certainly an issue you should consider when deciding exactly what and how much to make public on your site or elsewhere. This is a matter of ethics, but sometimes it might also be a legal matter (in some parts of the world it's literally against the law to publicize certain personal data).

Perhaps the best rule of thumb to use is the "Golden Rule." Ask yourself if you would want someone else to include certain details about *you* in public. If your answer is no, don't include those details about other living individuals unless you have their express permission to do so.

Mommy in the Bank

For personal security, don't use your mother's maiden name as part of your ID. Make one up!

For more information on why Internet privacy is important, see Jo Mitchell's "Privacy Issues" on her site, Cregan Ancestry (*homepages.rootsweb.com/~cregan/privacy.htm*). For some really scary stuff, see Identity Theft at *identitytheft.org* (shown in the following figure). There's no need to be paranoid in cyberspace, but a good dose of caution is a great idea.

Learn how to protect yourself and others.

Build a Genealogy Web Site

If I haven't scared you off, let's get down to business. Review your checklist and storyboard, and make any necessary final modifications. Well, I say "final," but you'll probably want to change a few things later. Just as a family tree is never truly finished, Web sites tend to keep growing and evolving, too. But like your research itself, the process of building a Web site has to begin *somewhere*!

For general reference and more information on how to put your family tree online, you might want to bookmark the following sites.

- Genealogy Web Page Tutorial at *www.geocities.com/ Heartland/Acres/7002/* (shown in the following figure)

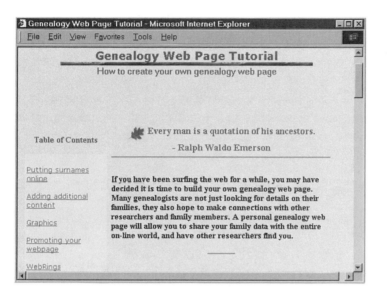

This multi-part tutorial explains several aspects of building genealogy sites.

- Cyndi Howells' "Genealogy Home Page Construction Kit" at *www.cyndislist.com/construc.htm* (shown in the following figure)

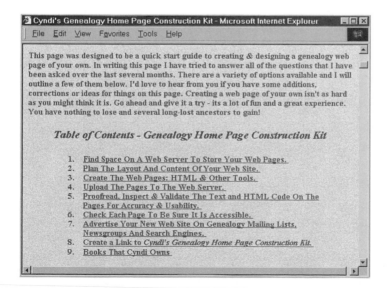

Several types of resources on one page for quick reference.

Let Your Software Do the Work

Even if you know very little or no HTML (Hypertext Markup Language, the "code" that tells Web browsers how to translate page formatting), software can make your task easy. Check to see if your genealogy database software offers options to generate reports in HTML format (it might even make an entire "instant Web site" based on your data).

Prettier Pages

If "plain vanilla" pages seem too boring, it only takes a little basic HTML to add flavor. Learn more online!

You can see sites created by users of Ultimate Family Tree software at *www.uftree.com/UFT/Nav/familywebpagesview.html*, and Family Tree Maker users can easily produce sites similar to the one shown in the following figure. Other software makers provide Web capabilities, too. Each is different, so consult your software's manual and Help section for details on how to put it to work.

Links to ancestral reports and other data are further down this page.

If your genealogy software can't make Web pages, you're still ahead of the game if you use it to create GEDCOM files (most modern software titles have this capability). There are numerous shareware and freeware utilities that will convert GEDCOMs into HTML formatted pages. You'll be responsible for getting them online, and you might want to add extra formatting to make them more attractive. But these utilities can produce HTML files very quickly, which means the bulk of your genealogy site can be constructed in mere minutes.

You can see more examples of pages created with various software and utilities (plus links for obtaining them) at *www. geocities.com/Heartland/Acres/7002/gc2gedcom.html*. At this site you can also learn more about utilities (such as GEDClean and GEDliving) that will automatically "strip" data about living individuals from your GEDCOM. You can do this manually, but such a utility can save you hours, especially on a large GEDCOM file.

Use Online Web-Builders

If you have a GEDCOM file but don't want to convert it to HTML and upload it to the Web, you're still in luck! There are some sites that can save you the work—that is, if you require only a basic site; there's nothing fancy about these. One example is Dave Wilks' free GEDCOM server at *www.my-ged.com*. Follow the easy instructions to send your GEDCOM by email, and Mr. Wilks will do the work for you—for free. The resulting individual sites are simple but attractive (the following figure shows an example of one individual's "Coverpage").

Keep It Fresh

To keep your site from getting stale, periodically check links and make changes, even if only minor ones.

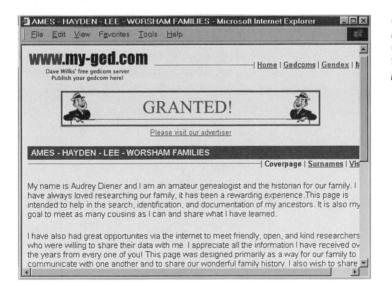

One user's my-ged.com site (links to data are further down the page).

How about a family tree chart you can build "on-the-fly?" You might like to try FamilyExplorer's "Instant Family Tree" at *www.genealogy.com/genealogy/familyexplorer*. You must have a Java-enabled Web browser to use and view this, and there are a few drawbacks (for example, it only allows one marriage per individual). But it's a fun and easy way to get a simple family tree chart online. I created an example using a bit of my own genealogy data, which you can see at *www.genealogy.com/users/l/a/m/Terri-E-Lamb/ftitree.html* (shown in the following figure) .

A tiny branch of my family tree as a Java-based chart.

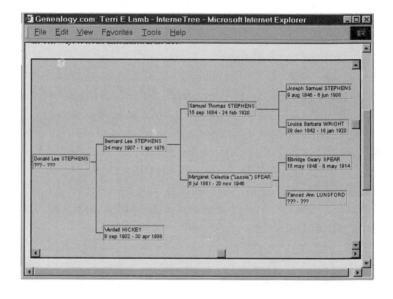

Make a Splash

But don't go overboard to do so. Avoid unsightly clutter; don't try to use every fancy idea you find.

If your primary interest is to exchange data and information privately only among people of your own choosing, you might want to create a site at MyFamily.com (*www.myfamily.com*). These sites are easy to make, and they're completely private, because user names and passwords are required for viewing. It's up to you to decide who gets to be a member. I didn't create the example you can view, but you can access it without a password by clicking on the Sample Site link (a portion of the site is shown in the following figure). You can keep in touch with long-distance family members by using your own chat room and "news" area, plus you can easily upload photos, GEDCOMs, or other files to share.

MyFamily.com's Sample Site shows what you can do with yours.

If you want to use HTML files generated by your software and/or utilities or that you created yourself, getting them online isn't as complicated as you may think. There are several servers online that provide free Web space as well as easy-to-use online tools to get your family tree online. If you want, you can create a site from scratch (following your storyboard), even without any previously existing HTML files. The following list shows just a few of these servers (you can find others by using your Web search skills).

www.channel21.com

www.50megs.com

www.freeservers.com

www.quikpages.com

www.netcolony.com

www.webjump.com

www.webspawner.com

Other Ways to Build a Site

If you already have a personal site, you might want to add your genealogy data on new pages you can upload to your existing site. Then again, you might want a separate and distinct site just for your genealogy information and data. Or maybe you don't have a site yet, but you want more control and creative options than the "easy-builder" type servers allow.

In your case is similar to the previous scenarios, you'll probably want an HTML editor and FTP (file transfer protocol) software. It really isn't difficult to create your own site pages or to learn to upload and maintain them. I don't have room to go into detail here, but there are lots of wonderful resources online where you can learn more. Your hometown ISP might also be able to help you, so don't hesitate to call them and ask. The following sites should lead you to just about anything you ever wanted to know about creating Web sites and putting them online.

Ultimate HTML

If you'd like to get into the real nitty-gritty and also get great site ideas, see *hwg.org*.

netforbeginners.about.com

personalweb.about.com

webdesign.about.com

html.about.com

The Bottom Line

If you skipped to this chapter to learn how to build a genealogy site, be sure to review earlier chapters in order to develop a solid basis for all of your research. If you've read all the chapters and practiced the skills you learned, well done! In addition to some possible surprises you might have learned in this chapter, you should know

- To make and follow a good "blueprint" as you construct your genealogy Web site.

- How to avoid breaking the law (even by accident), and some steps you can take to ensure privacy for living individuals.

- How software can help you build your site.

- Some ways to build a quick and easy genealogy site, and how to learn more about Web site design.

Workshop

Use the following workshop to help reinforce the knowledge
you've gained in this lesson.

**Q If someone shares data with me by email, can I use it on
my Web site?**

A You can use the data itself as long as you change the way it
is presented (remember to cite your source and add a note if
the data isn't verified). Don't quote the email verbatim without the correspondent's express permission.

**Q I saw the cutest picture of Bugs Bunny on another per-
sonal site. Can I use it on my site?**

A Probably not. Just because the graphic was on another personal site, it doesn't mean it was used legally. You could vio-
late copyright and trademark laws if you use it without
proper permission (from the rightful owner of the graphic,
not just the other Web site owner).

**Q I'm extremely new to computers and the Internet. Can I
learn to make a genealogy Web site?**

A You might want to wait a while so you can gain more experience, but it's not as hard as it looks. If you want to jump in,
be sure to go slowly and keep it simple at first.

Quiz

Take the following quiz to see how much you've learned.

Questions

1. True or False: It's okay to copy a post made on a public
   forum. (Hint: use a Web site mentioned in this chapter to help
   you find the answer.)

2. Name at least three elements no personal genealogy site's
   main page should be without.

3. True or False: You don't need special software to build
   genealogy Web sites.

4. True or False: It's possible to build an attractive site even if
   you don't know HTML.

Answers

1. False. While it's acceptable to copy public forum messages for your private perusal, it is not okay to reproduce them for other public presentation without the express consent of the author.

2. An informative title, a description of what's on the site, an index (links) to other parts of the site, a list of major surnames, latest modification date, Web author's name, author's email address. (Did you think of others not named here?)

3. True. Genealogy software, related utilities, and other types of software can help make your task easier, but you can also build a site without them.

4. True. There are many online tools that will guide you as you go.

PART V

Appendixes

APPENDIX A

Recommended Sites

Use the Web sites listed in this appendix, along with techniques described throughout this book, to research your family tree. This list represents only a tiny fraction of what you'll find online, but you'll be off to a great start.

General Directories & Search Engines

About.com	*home.about.com*
Alta Vista	*www.altavista.com*
Beaucoup!	*www.beaucoup.com*
BigHub.com	*www.thebighub.com*
Excite	*www.excite.com*
Go Network	*www.go.com*
Google!	*www.google.com*

The Google search engine at www.google.com.

GoTo.com	www.goto.com
HotBot	www.hotbot.com
LookSmart	www.looksmart.com
Lycos Network	www.lycos.com
whatUseek	whatUseek.com
Yahoo!	www.yahoo.com

Getting Organized

Abstracts for census records
www.familytreemaker.com/00000061.html

Adobe Acrobat Reader
www.adobe.com/products/acrobat/readermain.html

Ancestry.com Charts and Forms
ancestry.com/download/forms.htm

Ancestry Corner
www.ancestrycorner.com

Find forms on Ancestry Corner, at www.ancestrycorner.com.

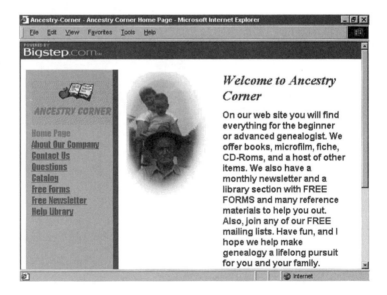

Form Letters and Other Aids
www.familytreemaker.com/00000023.html

How to Protect and Store Photos, Documents & Works of Art
members.aol.com/lredtail/Kevins.html

Organization of Genealogical Materials
www.rootsweb.com/~ote/organize.htm

Twenty Ways to Avoid Genealogical Grief
www.rootsweb.com/roots-l/20ways.html

History, Genealogy, and Geography Resources

About.com Genealogy
genealogy.about.com

About.com Geography
geography.about.com

About.com's history section
home.about.com/education/history

American Life Histories
memory.loc.gov/ammem/wpaintro/wpahome.html

American Memory collection
memory.loc.gov/ammem/ammemhome.html

Ancestry.com
ancestry.com

Cyndi's List
www.cyndislist.com

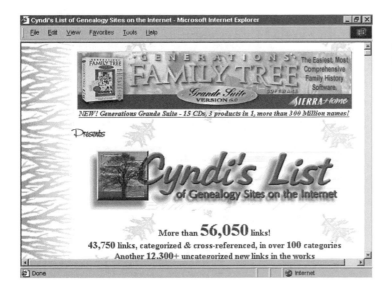

Cyndi's List (www.cyndislist. com) offers one-stop access to many genealogy resources.

DearMYRTLE's Genealogy for Beginners
www.ancestry.com/lessons/beginners/beginners.htm

Genealogy.com
www.genealogy.com

The Genealogy Web Portal
surnameweb.org

Geographic Names Information System
mapping.usgs.gov/www/gnis

TheHistoryNet
thehistorynet.com

The History Place
historyplace.com

Maps and Gazetteers
www.ancestry.com/ancestry/maps.asp

Railroad Maps
memory.loc.gov/ammem/gmdhtml/rrhtml/rrhome.html

RootsWeb
www.rootsweb.com

RootsWeb.com offers another good all-purpose starting point.

The Source: A Guidebook of American Genealogy
ancestry.com/home/source/srcindex.htm

U.S. GenWeb Project
www.usgenweb.org

U.S. Geological Survey
www.usgs.gov

U.S. Library of Congress
www.loc.gov

Finding Your Family Online

Ancestry World Tree
www.ancestry.com/worldtree/tree.htm

Books We Own
www.rootsweb.com/~bwo

FamilySearch
familysearch.org

Family Surname Websites and Associations
www.angelfire.com/ks/windshipgenhelp/family.html

GenConnect
cgi.rootsweb.com/~genbbs

GENDEX
www.gendex.com/gendex

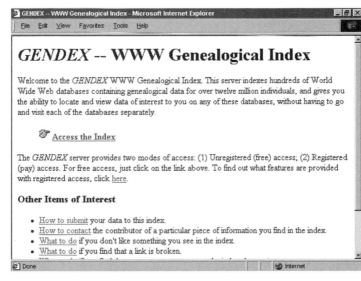

GENDEX (www.gendex.com/gendex) connects you to records covering over 12 million people.

Genealogical CDs
genweb.net/~gen-cds/cdlist.html

The Genealogy Helplist
posom.com/hl

Genealogy's Most Wanted
www.citynet.net/mostwanted

GenForum
genforum.familytreemaker.com

GenServ
www.genserv.com

The Guild of One-Name Studies
www.one-name.org

Internet Family Finder
www.familytreemaker.com/allsearch.html

Mailing Lists
members.aol.com/johnf14246/gen_mail.html

Personal Home Pages
www.cyndislist.com/personal.htm

Relatively Seeking
www.the-seeker.com/relative.htm

Society Hill directory
www.daddezio.com/society

User Mailing Lists Hosted by RootsWeb
www.rootsweb.com/~maillist

Weekly Genealogy Chat
www.daddezio.com/genealogy/chat.html

www.my-ged.com
www.my-ged.com

D'Addezio (www.daddezio. com) offers a weekly genealogy chat.

Name Resources

Books on Modern Names
www.s-gabriel.org/docs/modnames.html

Canada GenWeb
www.rootsweb.com/~canwgw

General Name References
www.s-gabriel.org/docs/gennames.html

The Genealogy Web Portal
surnameweb.org

GeneaNet
www.autumnstar.com/GeneaNet

The Guild of One-Name Studies
www.one-name.org

Learn everything about one-name studies through The Guild at www.one-name.org.

Nicknames and Naming Traditions
www.tngenweb.usit.com/franklin/frannick.htm

Our Ancestors' Nicknames
www.uftree.com/UFT/HowTos/SettingOut/nickname1.html

Surname Resources at RootsWeb
resources.rootsweb.com/surnames

U.S. Surname Distribution
www.hamrick.com/names

What's In a Name?
clanhuston.com/name/name.htm

World GenWeb
worldgenweb.org

Online Records Resources

ALGenWeb Archives Land and Deed Records
www.rootsweb.com/~algwarch/land_deed.htm

Ancestry.com's SSDI
www.ancestry.com/ancestry/search/ssdi/ssdi_index.asp

Bureau of Land Management
www.glorecords.blm.gov

The official Bureau of Land Management site (www.glorecords.blm.gov) lets you browse through two million land titles.

Census Online
www.census-online.com/links

ClassMates.com
www.classmates.com

Immigrant Ships Transcribers Guild
istg.rootsweb.com

IOOF Family History Research
www.ioof.org/IOOF/FamilyResearch.html

KnowX.com (Public Records)
www.knowx.com

Letters From Forgotten Ancestors
www.tngenweb.usit.com/tnletters

Lost and Found
www.cyndislist.com/photos.htm

Military Resources Worldwide
www.cyndislist.com/milres.htm

NARA's Genealogy Page
www.nara.gov/genealogy

National Archives and Records Administration
www.nara.gov

Newspaper Association of America
www.naa.org/hotlinks

Religion and Churches
www.cyndislist.com/religion.htm

"Research in Church Records" (*The Source: A Guidebook of American Genealogy*)
www.ancestry.com/home/source/src124.htm

Social Security Records
www.ancestry.com/research/ssdi.htm

University of Kentucky's Oral History Program
www.uky.edu/Libraries/Special/oral_history

Learn what was said then, on the U of Kentucky's Oral History site at www.uky.edu/Libraries/Special/oral_history.

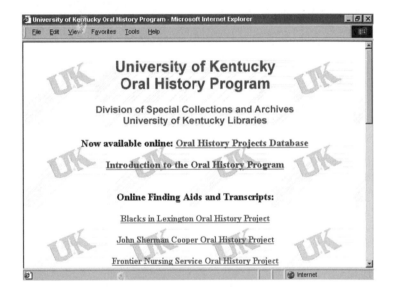

USGenWeb Archives Project
www.rootsweb.com/~usgenweb

USGenWeb Census Project FAQ
www.rootsweb.com/~usgwcens/help/questions.html

USGenWeb Tombstone Transcription Project
www.rootsweb.com/~cemetery

Vital Records Information
vitalrec.com

Religious, Ethnic, and Other Special Resources

Abbreviations Found in Genealogy
www.rootsweb.com/~rigenweb/abbrev.html

About.com Women's History
womenshistory.about.com

Adoption Search Basics for Beginners
adoption.about.com/library/weekly/aa062199.htm

The African-Native Genealogy Homepage
members.aol.com/angelaw859

American Popular Music Before 1900
www.nhmccd.edu/contracts/lrc/kc/music-1.html

AmeriSpeak
www.rootsweb.com/~genepool/amerispeak.htm

AOL Hispanic Genealogy SIG
users.aol.com/mrosado007

A Belle of the Fifties
metalab.unc.edu/docsouth/clay/clay.html

Christine's Genealogy Website
www.ccharity.com

Chronology, Era, and Calendars
www.bdl.fr/Granpub/calendriers_eng.html

Deciphering Old Handwriting
www.firstct.com/fv/oldhand.html

Female Ancestry
www.ancestry.com/magazine/articles/female.htm

Glossary of Diseases
www.rootsweb.com/~ote/disease.htm

JewishGen Family Finder
www.jewishgen.org/jgff

If you have Jewish ancestors, the JewishGen Family Finder (www. jewishgen.org/ jgff) can help you track down their place of origin.

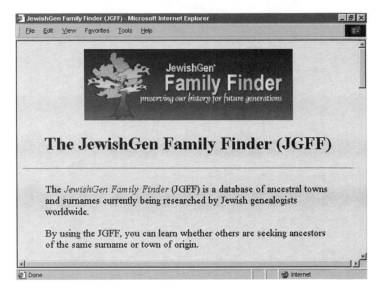

Leon's Political Almanac
www.magnolia.net/~leonf/cgi/hypercal.cgi

A List of Occupations
cpcug.org/user/jlacombe/terms.html

Native American resources
www.cyndislist.com/native.htm

Old Handwriting Samples
www.rootsweb.com/~ote/writing.htm

Orphan Train Heritage Society of America, Inc.
pda.republic.net/othsa

Project Gutenberg
promo.net/pg

Recipes, Cookbooks, and Family Traditions
www.cyndislist.com/recipes.htm

Religion and Churches
www.cyndislist.com/religion.htm

"Research in Church Records" (*The Source: A Guidebook of American Genealogy*)
www.ancestry.com/home/source/src124.htm

Some Historically Significant Epidemics
www.botany.duke.edu/microbe/chrono.htm

Check out when and where that epidemic hit, on the *Historically Significant Epidemics* page at www.botany.duke. edu/microbe/ chrono.htm.

Some Important Epidemics - Microsoft Internet Explorer

File　Edit　View　Favorites　Tools　Help

Some Historically Significant Epidemics

480 B.C. The Plague of Xerxes, probably an outbreak of dysentery, hit the Persian army, facilitating its defeat by the Greeks. The Greek historian Herodotus probably exaggerated its impact, but it is nonetheless significant as one of the first epidemics recorded in a lengthy written account.

451 B.C. A severe outbreak of an unidentified disease struck Rome, and was recorded by the historians Livy and Dionysius of Halicarnasus.

430 B.C. The Great Plague of Athens was described by Thucydides, who survived an attack himself. The symptoms described have been variously interpreted as smallpox, typhus, bubonic plague, or most recently, Ebola virus. The outbreak seriously impaired the Athenian army, and prolonged the Peloponnesian War.

410 B.C. The first recorded epidemic of mumps was described by Hippocrates, who was probably present on the Island of Thasos where the epidemic struck around 410.

400 B.C. Hippocrates also recorded an outbreak of a cough followed by pneumonia and other symptoms, at Perinthus in northern Greece (now part of Turkey). Several possible identifications have been suggested, including influenza, whooping cough and diphtheria.

Done

Texas Coalition for Adoption Reform & Education
www.visualimage.com/txcare/history.html

USGenWeb Tombstone Transcription Project
www.rootsweb.com/~cemetery

Software
Adobe Systems, Inc.
www.adobe.com

Ancestors and Descendants
www.aia-and.com

Ancestral Quest
www.ancestralquest.com

Brother's Keeper
ourworld.compuserve.com/homepages/Brothers_Keeper

Clooz
www.ancestordetective.com/clooz.htm

Cumberland Family Tree
www.cf-software.com

Family Matters
www.matterware.com

Family Matters is one of many genealogy software programs; learn more at www.matterware. com.

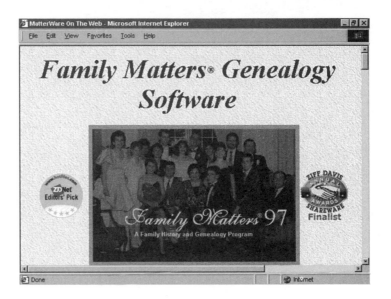

Family Origins
members.aol.com/famorigins

Family Reunion
www.famware.com

Family Treasures
www.famtech.com/FamilyTres.htm

Family Tree Maker
www.familytreemaker.com

GED2HTML
www.gendex.com/ged2html

GED2WEB
www.oramwt.demon.co.uk/GED2WEB/ged2web.htm

GED2WWW
www.lesandchris.com/ged2www

GED Browser
www.misbach.org/gedbrowser

GEDClean32
www.raynorshyn.com/gedclean

The GEDCOM Standard Release 5.5
www.tiac.net/users/pmcbride/gedcom/55gctoc.htm

GEDCOM Utilities
www.rootsweb.com/~gumby/ged.html

gedcomToHTML
www.bath.ac.uk/~enpdp/Gedcom/gedcomToHTML.html

GedHTree
www.users.uswest.net/~gwel/gedhtree.htm

GEDitCOM
www.xmission.com/~geditcom

GEDPAGE
www.frontiernet.net/~rjacob/gedpage.htm

GEDPrivy
hometown.aol.com/gedprivy

GeDStrip
webhome.idirect.com/~naylor/gedstrip.htm

GEDTable
www.cobnet.com/Programs/GEDTable

GenDesigner
www.gendesigner.com

Genealogy Software SpringBoard
www.gensoftsb.com

Genealogy Web Page Tutorial: Gedcoms
www.geocities.com/Heartland/Acres/7002/gc2gedcom.html

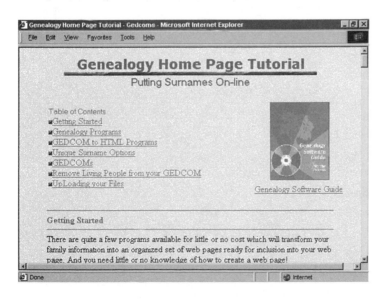

The Genealogy Home Page Tutorial (www. geocities.com/ Heartland/Acres/ 7002/gc2gedcom. html) makes your family home page a snap.

Gene Macintosh
www.ics.uci.edu/~eppstein/gene

GeneWeb
cristal.inria.fr/~ddr/GeneWeb

Generations Family Tree
www.sierra.com/sierrahome/familytree/titles/gengs

Heritage
www.eskimo.com/~grandine/heritage.html

HTML Genie
www.geneaware.com/products.html

Use HTML Genie (www.geneaware. com/products. html) to convert your GEDCOM data into a fast, easy Web page.

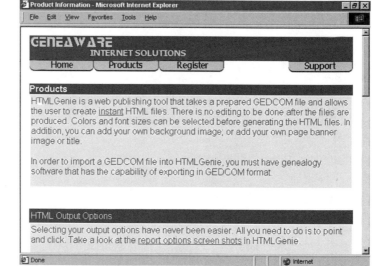

JavaGED
www.sc3.net/JavaGEDHome.html

Kinship Archivist
kinshiparchivist.com

Legacy Family Tree
www.legacyfamilytree.com

LifeLines
www.bartonstreet.com/software/lines

The Master Genealogist
www.whollygenes.com

Parents
ourworld.compuserve.com/homepages/NickleWare

Personal Ancestral File
www.familysearch.org/OtherResources/paf4

Relatives
mypage.direct.ca/v/vdouglas/RelIntro.html

Reunion
www.leisterpro.com

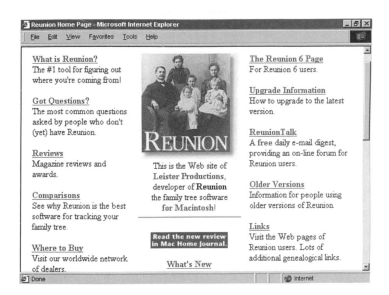

There's genealogy software for the Mac, too—see Reunion at www. leisterpro.com.

RootsView
home.earthlink.net/~naturalsoft/rootsview.htm

Sparrowhawk
www.bradandkathy.com/genealogy/sparrowhawk.html

TreeBuilder
pw2.netcom.com/~rrao/familytree.html

uFTi
www.ufti.demon.co.uk/homepage.htm

Ultimate Family Tree
www.uftree.com

WebGED: Progenitor
www.access.digex.net/~giammot/webged

Your Family Tree Online
10 Big Myths
www.templetons.com/brad/copymyths.html

Visit www.
templetons.com/
brad/copymyths.
html *to separate
copyright myth
from reality.*

50Megs.com
www.50megs.com

About.com's HTML
html.about.com

About.com's Internet for Beginners
netforbeginners.about.com

About.com's Personal Web Pages
personalweb.about.com

About.com's Web Design
webdesign.about.com

channel21.com
www.channel21.com

Copyright & Fair Use
fairuse.stanford.edu

FamilyExplorer's "Instant Family Tree"
www.genealogy.com/genealogy/familyexplorer

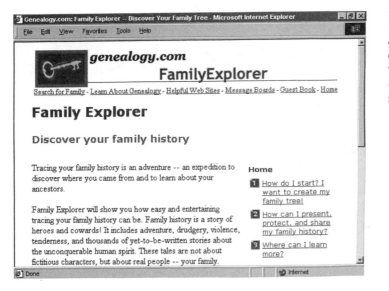

The Instant Family Tree (www.genealogy.com/genealogy/familyexplorer) makes it easy to get started.

Family Tree of Terri E. Lamb
www.genealogy.com/users/l/a/m/Terri-E-Lamb/ftitree.html

Freeservers.com
www.freeservers.com

GEDCOM Utilities
www.rootsweb.com/~gumby/ged.html

Genealogy Home Page Construction Kit
www.cyndislist.com/construc.htm

Genealogy Web Page Tutorial
www.geocities.com/Heartland/Acres/7002/

MyFamily.com
www.myfamily.com

*Get all your
family members
hooked together
via MyFamily.com.*

My-GED
www.my-ged.com

NetColony
www.netcolony.com

Privacy Issues
homepages.rootsweb.com/~cregan/privacy.htm

Ultimate Family Tree user pages
www.uftree.com/UFT/Nav/familywebpagesview.html

U.S. Copyright and Genealogy
www.rootsweb.com/~mikegoad/copyright.htm

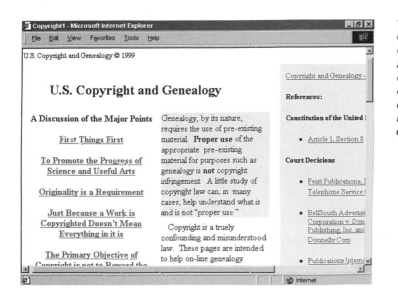

This U.S. Copyright and Genealogy page at www.rootsweb.com/~mikegoad/copyright.htm offers no-nonsense legal explanations.

WebJump
www.webjump.com

Webspawner
www.webspawner.com

APPENDIX B

Sources Checklist

Use this checklist as both a guide to genealogical sources and a reminder to check for possible clues you might find on the Web or around your home, at courthouses, libraries, or other repositories.

Birth

___ Adoption records

___ Baby books

___ Baby gift registries

___ Baby shower rosters

___ Biographies

___ Birth announcements

___ Birth certificates

___ Birthday cards

___ Census records

___ Church records

___ Death records

___ Employment records

___ Family Bibles

___ Family records

___ Financial records

___ Grave markers

___ Health/Medical records

___ Hospital records

___ Marriage records

___ Memorabilia

___ Military records

___ Newspaper clippings

___ Obituaries

___ Personal records

___ Photographs

___ Prison records

___ School records

___ Wills

Church and Religion

___ Bar/Bat Mitzvah records

___ Baptismal records

___ Bibles

___ Blessings

___ Catechism records

___ Cemetery registries

___ Church financial records

___ Church histories

___ Church membership directories

___ Church minutes

___ Church/Religious publications

___ Christening records

___ Confirmation records

___ Denominational timelines

___ Disciplinary records

___ Donation records

___ Family records

___ Grave markers

___ Health/Medical records

___ Hymnals

___ Memorabilia

___ Military records

___ Ministerial records

___ Newspaper clippings

___ Obituaries

___ Ordination records

___ Pamphlets

___ Parish records

___ Personal records

___ Photographs

___ Prayer books

___ Rabbinical records

___ Religious garments

___ Religious timelines

___ Sealings

___ Seminary records

___ Sunday school records

___ Synagogue records

Civil and Legal

___ Arrest records

___ Bonds

___ Bounty awards

___ Citizenship papers

___ Contracts

___ Court records

___ Deportation papers

___ Employment records

___ Guardianship papers

___ Land and property records

___ Licenses

___ Memorabilia

___ Newspaper clippings

___ Obituaries

___ Personal records

___ Photographs

___ Prison records

___ Probate records

___ School records

___ Summons

___ Subpoenas

___ Tax records

___ Traffic violation tickets

___ Voter registration records

___ Wills

Death

___ Burial announcements

___ Burial records

___ Cemetery records

___ Church records

___ Death certificates

___ Disease/Illness timelines

___ Family Bibles

___ Funeral records

___ Grave markers

___ Hospital records

___ Medical records

___ Memorial books

___ Military records

___ Newspaper clippings

___ Obituaries

___ Personal records

___ Photographs

___ Prison records

___ Social Security benefit records

___ Sympathy cards

___ Wills

Employment and Occupation

___ Achievement awards

___ Apprenticeship records

___ Business/Industry publications

___ Business/Industry timelines

___ Census records

___ Citations

___ Disability records

___ Disciplinary records

___ Health/Medical records

___ Income tax records

___ Insurance records

___ Letters/Memoranda

___ Licenses/Certifications

___ Memorabilia

___ Military records

___ Newspaper clippings

___ Obituaries

___ Occupation timelines

___ Pension records

___ Personal records

___ Photographs

___ Prison records

___ Promotions

___ Relocation records

___ Resumes/Work histories

___ Retirement records

___ Transfer records

___ School records

___ Severance records

___ Social Security applications

___ Social Security cards

___ Union records

___ Wage records

Family

___ Audio/Video records

___ Bibles

___ Biographies

___ Books

___ Bulletins

___ Census records

___ Charts/Pedigrees

___ Crests/Coats of arms

___ Ethnic/Religious customs

___ Genealogies/Histories

___ Health/Medical records

___ Heirlooms

___ Memorabilia

___ Military records

___ Newsletters

___ Newspaper clippings

___ Personal records

___ Photographs

___ Stories

___ Traditions

Health and Medical

___ Adoption records

___ Admission/Discharge notices

___ Birth records

___ Death records

___ Disease/Illness timelines

___ Employment records

___ Ethnic/Religious records

___ "Get Well" cards

___ Hospital records

___ Immigration/Naturalization records

___ Immunization records

___ Insurance papers

___ Medical history

___ Military infirmary records

___ Newspaper clippings

___ Notes from doctors/nurses

___ Obituaries

___ Personal records

___ Photographs

___ Prescriptions

___ Prison infirmary records

___ School infirmary records

___ Vaccination records

___ Wills

___ X-ray films

Household

___ Collectibles

___ Dishes

___ Drawings/Paintings

___ Embroidered items

___ Engraved items

___ Gifts

___ Heirlooms

___ Linens

___ Monogrammed clothing

___ Needlework

___ Newspaper clippings

___ Personal records

___ Photographs

___ Plaques

___ Quilts

___ Recipes

___ Samplers

___ Silverware

___ Souvenirs

___ Tapestries

Immigration and Citizenship

___ Airplane/Ship manifests

___ Alien registration papers

___ Birth records

___ Census records

___ Church records

___ Citizenship applications

___ Death records

___ Deportment papers

___ Emigration patterns

___ Employment records

___ Ethnic/Religious records

___ Grave markers

___ Health/Medical records

___ Immigration timelines

___ Marriage records

___ Memorabilia

___ Migration trails

___ Military records

___ Naturalization papers

___ Newspaper clippings

___ Obituaries

___ Passports

___ Personal records

___ Photographs

___ Prison records

___ Relocation records

___ School records

___ Ship passenger lists

___ Visas

___ Wills

Land and Property

___ Abstracts of Title

___ Appraisal records

___ Census records

___ Deeds

___ Estate records

___ Financial records

___ Homestead certificates

___ Land grants

___ Land lottery timelines

___ Landlord records

___ Leases

___ Marriage/Divorce records

___ Mortgage records

___ Newspaper clippings

___ Obituaries

___ Personal records

___ Photographs

___ Relocation records

___ Tax assessments

___ Tax notices

___ Tax records

___ Tenant records

___ Water/Mineral rights

___ Wills

Licenses and Certificates

___ Alcohol sales

___ Attorney

___ Birth

___ Death

___ Driver/Vehicle operator

___ Employment records

___ Family records

___ Financial advisor

___ Firearms

___ Fishing

___ General business

___ Hunting

___ Marriage

___ Medical

___ Newspaper clippings

___ Obituaries

___ Other business

___ Other occupational

___ Other professional

___ Personal records

___ Private motor vehicle

___ Public motor vehicle

___ Public transportation

___ Real estate agent/broker

___ Teacher

___ Tobacco sales

___ Securities broker

___ Wills

Marriage and Divorce

___ Anniversary announcements

___ Anniversary cards

___ Annulment papers

___ Census records

___ Church records

___ Death/Burial records

___ Divorce papers

___ Employment records

___ Marriage certificates

___ Memorabilia

___ Military records

___ Newspaper clippings

___ Obituaries

___ Personal records

___ Photographs

___ Prison records

___ Tax records

___ Wedding announcements

___ Wedding books

___ Wedding cards

___ Wedding gift registries

___ Wedding shower rosters

___ Wills

Military

___ Battle timelines

___ Census records

___ Church records

___ Citations

___ Disability records

___ Discharge records

___ Disciplinary records

___ Employment records

___ Enlistment records

___ Firearms

___ Infirmary records

___ Insignias

___ Memorabilia

___ Muster rolls

___ National Guard/Reserve records

___ Newspaper clippings

___ Obituaries

___ Pension records

___ Personal records

___ Photographs

___ Promotions

___ Recruitment records

___ Ribbons

___ Selective Service records

___ Service medals

___ Swords

___ Uniforms

___ War timelines

___ Wills

Personal

___ Audio/Video records

___ Autograph albums

___ Bank records

___ Bibles

___ Bills/Invoices

___ Biographies

___ Books

___ Certificates

___ Club/Lodge memberships

___ Cookbooks

___ Diaries

___ Ethnic/Religious records

___ Family scrapbooks

___ Financial records

___ Genealogies

___ Greeting cards

___ Health/Medical records

___ Housewarming records

___ Insurance records

___ Journals

___ Keepsakes/Mementos

___ Letters

___ Library cards

___ Licenses/Certificates

___ Newspaper clippings

___ Notes/Memoranda

___ Obituaries

___ Passports

___ Photographs

___ Plaques

___ Postcards

___ Receipts

___ Recipes

___ Relocation records

___ Stationery

___ Stories

___ Travelogues/Itineraries

___ Trophies

School

___ Band/Choir records

___ Census records

___ Certificates

___ Church records

___ Classmates

___ Club records

___ Conduct records

___ Dance invitations/keepsakes

___ Degrees

___ Diplomas

___ Disciplinary records

___ Drama/Performance Art records

___ Employment records

___ Grade transcripts

___ Graduation cards

___ Grants/Scholarships

___ Health/Medical records

___ Honor rolls

___ Memorabilia

___ Military records

___ Newspaper clippings

___ Obituaries

___ Other extracurricular awards/records

___ Photographs

___ Pennants

___ Personal records

___ Plaques

___ Prison records

___ Project awards/records

___ Report cards

___ Scholastic awards

___ School songs

___ School histories

___ Special achievement records

___ Special event programs

___ Sports awards/records

___ Teachers

___ Textbooks

___ Trophies

___ Uniforms

___ Wills

___ Yearbooks

Glossary

abstract—A summary of important points (as in the information contained in census records).

abt.—Abbreviation for *about*.

AF (see **Ancestral File**)

a.k.a.—*Also known as*.

ancestor—A person from whom you descend in a direct line.

Ancestral File—One of the world's largest collections of lineage-linked records, maintained by the LDS Church.

archive—A collection of documents and records of a government or organization; may also refer to a personal collection.

Ashkenazic Jews—Jews who settled in eastern and central Europe (from *ashkenaz*, German for *Hebrew*).

atlas-and-gazetteer—A collection of maps, charts, and other geographic material.

b.—Abbreviation for *born* or *birth*, depending on context.

bastard—A child born out of wedlock (both males and females).

b.d.—Abbreviation for *birth date*.

bef.—Abbreviation for *before*.

bet.—Abbreviation for *between*.

bibliography—A list of books about a particular topic.

b.p.—Abbreviation for *birth place*.

bulletin board (see **message board**).

c.—Abbreviation for *circa*.

ca.—Abbreviation for *circa*.

census—An official enumeration or list of persons.

Christian name—A person's first name (given name); a term often used regardless of whether the person is a member of a Christian congregation or population.

Church of Jesus Christ of Latter-Day Saints—A Christian denomination founded in America by Joseph Smith. Maintains the world's largest collection of genealogy databases and other family history resources, freely accessible worldwide.

circa—About or approximately; usually refers to a date.

Co.—Abbreviation for *County*, as in Hamilton Co., Tennessee.

d.—Abbreviation for *died* or *death*, depending on context.

decennial—Occurring every *ten* years.

deed—A document representing the transfer of property ownership; also, the act of transferring ownership.

descendant—One who is descended from a specific ancestor in a direct line.

diaspora—Greek word for *dispersion*, used to describe a geographical spreading out of a family or other group over time.

ditto—Means *the same as what came before*, as on a list with similar entries. Often abbreviated as *d*, *do*, or *"*.

div.—Abbreviation for *divorce* or *divorced*.

d/o—Abbreviation for *daughter of*.

double dating—A method of recording dates by which the year is recorded according to both the Julian and the Gregorian calendars.

e-Genealogy—Electronic genealogy research, using computers and the Internet.

emigrate—To leave one's place of origin to live elsewhere.

emoticon—A simple icon depicting an emotion; created with keyboard symbols, letters, and/or numbers. Used in various online communications.

enumerate—To count, as in a census.

family group record (or **sheet**)—A form or chart recording a man, his wife, and their children.

f/o—Abbreviation for *father of*.

forum (see **message board**)

gazetteer—A geographical dictionary or index that lists or describes towns and other places.

GEDCOM—*GE*nealogical *D*ata *COM*munications, a standard format for special text files to be imported and/or exported by most current genealogy software.

genealogy—The study of the origin and descent of a family.

GF—Abbreviation for grandfather.

GGF; Ggrandfather— Abbreviations for great-grandfather.

GGM; Ggrandmother—Abbreviations for great-grandmother.

GM—Abbreviation for grandmother.

given name (see **Christian name**)

Gregorian calendar—A "new style" calendar based on the Julian calendar, adopted by America in 1752.

IGI (see **International Genealogical Index**)

immigrate—To settle into a new place after leaving the place of origin.

International Genealogical Index—The world's largest collection of records with information about births, marriages, deaths, parents, and spouses, maintained by the LDS Church.

Julian calendar—An "old style" calendar originated at the time of Julius Caesar's rule.

junior—Denotes the younger of two people with the same first name (not always related to each other).

LDS Church (see **Church of Jesus Christ of Latter-Day Saints**)

listserv—An email discussion group.

m.—Abbreviation for *married* or *marriage*, depending on context; multiple marriages are abbreviated *m1.*, *m2.*, and so on.

maiden name—A woman's surname prior to marriage.

maternal—Related through the mother.

message board—A Web site where you can read messages and post replies to other people.

migrate—To move residences from one place to another.

migration trail—Regular routes made by travelers as they migrated from one place to another.

m/o—Abbreviation for *mother of.*

NARA—U.S. National Archives and Records Administration.

nd—Abbreviation for *no date.*

netiquette—Etiquette for the Internet.

newsgroup—A type of online discussion group that resides on a different type of server from email or Web pages.

obituary—An announcement or notice of a person's death, with biographical information in varying details.

one-name study—A detailed genealogical project involving the study of one surname and all its variant spellings; sometimes a worldwide project that disregards actual family relationships.

onomastics—The formal study of the origin of names (people and places).

ornamental name—A surname added to a given name based on a fanciful concoction or adapted from a combination of existing surnames.

paternal—Related through the father.

patronymics—A naming system in which a surname is based on the father's given name.

primary record—A record created at or very near the time of an event.

publish—To make public, as in putting family data on a Web site or on a message board.

repository—The location of a record or archive, as in a library, courthouse, or an Internet database.

secondary record—A record created or copied from other sources; also, a record of events by "hearsay" (as in a son's marriage mentioned in his father's will).

Sephardic Jews—Jews that settled in the Iberian Peninsula (from *sepharad*, Spanish for *Hebrew*).

senior—The older of two people with the same first name (not always related).

s/o—Abbreviation for *son of.*

Soundex—An index system for census records. A name is assigned an alphanumeric code based loosely on the sound of the name.

source—A person or record that supplies data or information.

spam—A slang term used to mean unsolicited bulk emails; often commercial in nature, but the term applies to *any* such mail.

surname—The name (usually the last) that a person shares with other members of the same family.

vital records—Birth, marriage, and death records created and maintained by government entities.

will—A legal document describing a person's wishes according to the disposition of property after his or her death.

WWW—Abbreviation for the Internet's *World Wide Web*; also, my personal "Who, where, and when?" method of research.

INDEX

Tell Us What You Think!

As the reader of this book, *you* are our most important critic and commentator. We value your opinion and want to know what we're doing right, what we could do better, what areas you'd like to see us publish in, and any other words of wisdom you're willing to pass our way.

I welcome your comments. You can email or write me directly to let me know what you did or didn't like about this book—as well as what we can do to make our books stronger.

Please note that I cannot help you with technical problems related to the topic of this book, and that due to the high volume of mail I receive, I might not be able to reply to every message.

When you write, please be sure to include this book's title and author as well as your name and phone or fax number. I will carefully review your comments and share them with the author and editors who worked on the book.

Email: *internet_sams@mcp.com*

Mail: Mark Taber
           Associate Publisher
           Sams Publishing
           201 West 103rd Street
           Indianapolis, IN 46290 USA